Quick Clicks
REFERENCE GUIDE

MICROSOFT®
WORD® 2007

CAREERTRACK

QuickClicks Word 2007 Reference Guide

© 2011, 2010 CareerTrack, a division of PARK University Enterprises, Inc. All rights reserved.

2nd Edition

No part of this book may be reproduced, stored in a retrieval system, or transmitted in any form or by any means, including electronic, mechanical, photocopying, recording, or scanning without prior written permission from CareerTrack, except as permitted under Sections 107 or 108 of the 1976 United States Copyright Act.

Litho U.S.A.

Distributed in the U.S. and Canada

For orders or more information, please contact our customer service department at 1-800-556-3009.

ISBN: 978-1-935041-88-7

Item # 32017

Trademarks

QuickClicks is a registered trademark of CareerTrack and is registered in the U.S. Patent and Trademark Office. Reproduction of any kind is unlawful.

Access, ClipArt, Excel, Microsoft, PivotChart, PivotTable, PowerPoint and Word are registered trademarks of Microsoft Corporation. All rights reserved.

All other trademarks are the property of their respective owners.

Disclaimer

Purchasers, readers, or users of this book agree to be bound by the following terms:

Information contained in this book has been obtained by CareerTrack from sources believed to be reliable. The subject matter of this book is constantly evolving, and the information provided in this book is not exhaustive. The advice and strategies contained within might not be suitable for every situation. It should not be used as a substitute for consulting with a qualified professional where professional assistance is required or appropriate, or where there may be any risk to health or property.

In no event will CareerTrack or any of its respective affiliates, distributors, employees, agents, content contributors, or licensors be liable or responsible for damages including direct, indirect, special, consequential, incidental, punitive, exemplary losses, or damages and expenses including business interruption, loss of profits, lost business, or lost savings.

For purposes of illustrating the concepts and techniques described in this book, the author has created fictitious names; mailing, e-mail, and internet addresses; phone and fax numbers; and similar information. Any resemblance of this fictitious data that is similar to an actual person or organization is unintentional and purely coincidental.

The *QuickClicks Reference Guide* series is dedicated to all of CareerTrack's devoted customers. Our customers' commitment to continuing education and professional development inspired the creation of the award-winning *Unlocking the Secrets* CD-ROM series and the *QuickClicks Reference Guide* series.

Thank you for your continued support!

Contents

Introduction vi
    Anatomy of a Tip vi
    Extras Include the Following vii
    Understanding Word 2007 viii
    Getting Around Word 2007 ix

Format
1. Adjust Line and Paragraph Spacing 2
2. Adjust Text Alignment and Tabs 6
3. Arrange Text in Columns 10
4. Apply Borders and Shading to Text or a Page 14
5. Apply Styles to Text 18
6. Insert a Numbered or Bulleted List 22
7. Apply a Consistent Look and Feel to a Document 26
8. Create a Custom Look and Feel to Use in Documents 28
9. Apply a Watermark to a Page 32

Illustrate
10. Insert and Customize WordArt 36
11. Insert a Picture or Piece of Clip Art 38
12. Edit an Image's Appearance 42
13. Stack and Group Images in a Document 46
14. Create a List of All Illustrations in a Document 50

Design
15. Insert Text Box 52
16. Add a Table to a Document 54
17. Format Table Borders, Layout, and Shading 56
18. Perform Calculations in a Table 62
19. Insert and Manage Stored Document Components 64
20. Insert Manual Page Breaks 66
21. Divide Document into Sections 68
22. Insert Text or an Image at the Top or Bottom of a Page 70

Annotate
23. Insert a Hyperlink in a Document 74

QuickClicks: Microsoft Word 2007

contents

24. Mark a Point in a Document for Future Access 78
25. Create a Table of Contents. 82
26. Create an Index 86
27. Create a Document Summary 90
28. Insert a Footnote or Endnote 92
29. Correctly Cite Sources in a Document. 94
30. Create a Table of Authorities 98

Accelerate
31. Customize the Quick Access Toolbar and Status Bar 102
32. Create Templates 104
33. Locate and Substitute Words, Formatting, Terms, and Objects
    in a Document 108
34. Use AutoCorrect to Save Time and Prevent Errors 112
35. Customize Spellcheck and Grammar Check Options 116
36. Create Custom Spellcheck Lists for Documents and Projects. 120
37. Record and Play Back a Series of Actions. 122

Collaborate
38. Apply Password Security to a Document 126
39. Add, Respond to, and Delete Reviewer Comments 130
40. Monitor, Accept, and Reject Edits to a Document 134
41. Identify the Difference between Two Documents 138
42. Import Data from an Excel Spreadsheet into a Document. 142
43. Use Data from an Excel Spreadsheet to Populate Fields in a
    Document 144
44. Create a PowerPoint Presentation from a Word Document 148
45. Create a Form with Fillable Fields 150

Appendices
A. Customize Your Copy of Microsoft Word 158
B. Save a Document to the Appropriate File Format 162
C. Formatting Options 164
D. Track Changes and Comments Options 168
E. Create and Use Digital Signatures. 172
F. Keyboard Shortcuts 174
G. Index 176

Introduction

Congratulations on your purchase of *QuickClicks: Microsoft Word 2007*. You have invested wisely in yourself and taken a step forward in your personal and professional development.

This reference guide is an important tool in your productivity toolbox. By effectively using the word processing functions within Microsoft Word, you will be able to maximize your efficiency. The tips in this reference guide are written for the user who has a basic understanding of word processing and at least one year of experience using other Microsoft Office applications.

Anatomy of a Tip

Each tip displays the tip title in the top left corner and the tip category in the top right, so you always know where you are and what you are learning. Each tip is written in plain English. Some tips will include a "What Microsoft Calls It" reference to help you perform more effective searches for additional feature capabilities in Microsoft's help system.

What Microsoft Calls It:

Each tip is assigned a difficulty value from one to four, with one circle representing the easiest tips and four circles representing the hardest.

Difficulty: ●○○○

All tips begin with a business scenario, identified as **PROBLEM**.

SOLUTION explains how the demonstrated feature might be used to solve the problem. A set of easy-to-understand instructions follows.

Letter callouts, **A**, point to important parts of the screen. The names of all selections and buttons are **bolded** and easy to find.

introduction

Extras Include the Following

Icon	Name	What it Means
	Bright Idea	Bright ideas provide additional information about Word or the features in question.
	Hot Tip	Hot Tips share related functions and features, or additional uses of the features and functions, to the one being demonstrated.
	Caution	Cautions draw attention to situations where you might find yourself tripped up by a particularly complicated operation, instances when making an incorrect choice will cause you more work to correct, or times when very similar options might be confusing.

There are two other bonuses that do not have miniature icons. They are displayed at the end of tips, where appropriate. These are:

Icon	Name	What it Means
	Options	Options represent places where there are two or more ways to accomplish a task or where two or more results might be obtained, depending on the choices you make. Option icons appear within the text and all relevant choices are next to the icon.
	Quickest Click	Quickest Clicks indicate there is a faster way to accomplish the same task taught in the tip. Shortcuts like this, though, may leave out important steps that help you understand the feature. Therefore, each tip teaches the most complete method for accomplishing a task, and a Microsoft Quickest Click appears if there is a faster option.

At the bottom of each page, you will see either a Continue or a Stop icon. These icons indicate whether a tip continues on the next page or if it is complete.

Introduction

Understanding Word 2007

Microsoft Word is a powerful, word-processing program that enables you to easily create, modify, and share documents for print, electronic, or online use. Word 2007 is more powerful than previous versions of Word because new features and a new interface have improved usability and efficiency.

Word users can produce simple documents, such as fax cover sheets, letters, and memos, as well as complex documents, such as reports, syllabi, proposals, and grant applications. Word 2007 interfaces with other Microsoft Office 2007 applications to create presentation materials (PowerPoint); personalized communication, such as letters and invitations (Excel); and printed calendars and agendas (Outlook).

Word 2007 is a powerful tool for a variety of users:

Teachers or Trainers: Create educational materials for online use (with a variety of options such as active link and graphic elements) and for print (with a variety of options for sectioning the material into chapters or modules, page numbering, and formatting).

Students: Create reports and documents, as well as bibliographies or works cited pages. Word 2007 provides automated formatting around standard writing styles used in most colleges and universities, including MLA and APA style.

Managers and Team Leads: Create interactive, linked work schedules and automated Quality Monitoring Forms, or document employee performance.

Small Business Owners: Create invoices, billing schedules, and marketing materials with Word 2007's powerful design and formatting tools.

Getting Around Word 2007

Items Seen in the Word Window

Microsoft Word works similarly to most other Microsoft Office 2007 applications in terms of window structure and basic functions.

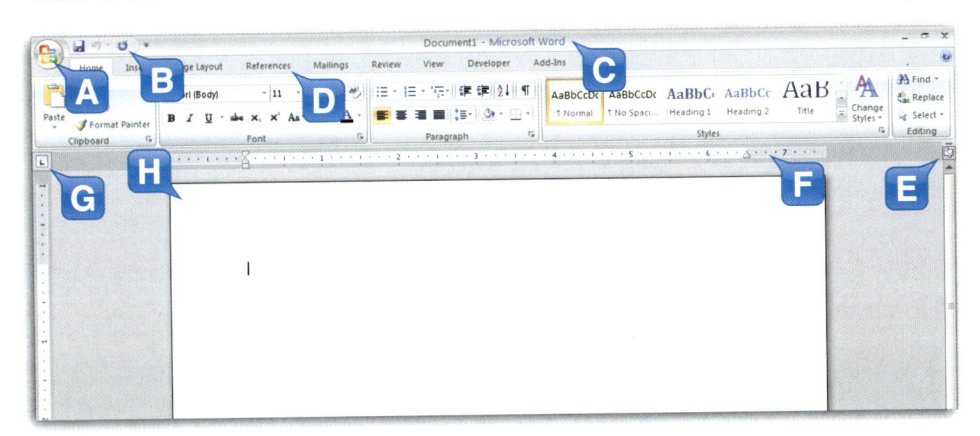

A Microsoft Office Button	Click this button to access the Windows Menu and locate the new, open, save, print, and other Word options.
B Quick Access Toolbar	Place items here for quick and easy access. The Save button is a default tool in the Quick Access toolbar. Click this button when you need to save your Word project.
C Title Bar	View the title and file type of the Word project.
D Ribbon/Tabs/ Groups	Locate Word menu items and controls.
E View Ruler Button **F** Ruler	Displays a horizontal ruler across the top of the document with markers for margins, indents, and tab stops.
G Tab Stop Selector	Marks the insertion point to stop at when you press the Tab key.
H Document Body	This is where your project text, objects, and graphics are displayed.

I Status Bar	The Status Bar is located at the bottom of the Word window and contains information such as page count, word count, view buttons, and a Zoom Slider.
J Zoom Slider	Zoom is the display size of a document within the document window. A higher zoom percentage (300%) makes everything appear larger, while a lower zoom percentage (50%) makes everything smaller. Use the plus and minus buttons to increase and decrease zoom.
K Page Up **L** Page Down Button	Click the Page Up button to view the previous page in the Document window. Click the Page Down button to view the next page in the Document window.
M Browse By Button	The Select Browse Object button brings up a menu that allows users to browse through the document by element or object type, including—for example—headings, comments, footnotes, and fields.

x   QuickClicks: Microsoft Word 2007

introduction

Print Preview Window

You can verify that the page is going to print the way you want by clicking Print Preview. This avoids printing multiple copies just to see what your project looks like. The Print Preview window shows you the exact placement of the data on each printed page. You can view all or part of your document.

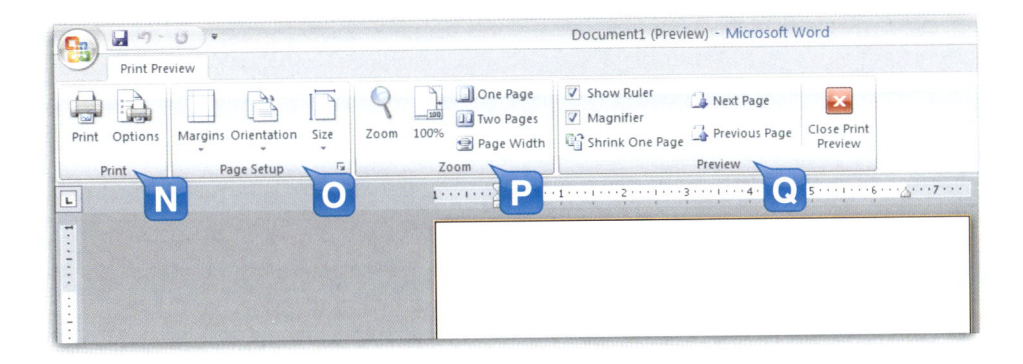

N Print		Select print options or click Print to open the Print Dialog box.
O Page Setup		Edit the margins, the page orientation, or size.
P Zoom		Click to zoom in and out to examine your document in the Preview window. Display pages one or two at a time and select how to fill the width of the preview window.
Q Preview		Preview options control what you see in the preview window—Ruler and Magnifier for example. The "Shrink One Page" option tells Word to attempt to reduce the document by one page by changing the font and spacing size. If you close the print preview window, you will return to the regular document window.

Introduction   xi

TIPS

1 Adjust Line and Paragraph Spacing

Difficulty: ●○○○

PROBLEM You need to present an outline of your department's annual goals to the Vice President. Your manager recommends that this presentation be one page only. The first draft of your document is more than a page. However, there is a lot of empty space that you can eliminate to reduce the document to a single page.

SOLUTION **Line Spacing** establishes the amount of vertical space between the lines of text in a paragraph. **Paragraph Spacing** establishes the amount of space above or below a paragraph. Microsoft Word 2007 sets default line spacing at 1.15 points and default paragraph spacing at 10 points. There are many instances when you may need to adjust this spacing to be larger or smaller, depending how the document will be used.

Step-by-Step

Adjust Line Spacing

1. Highlight the text you want to adjust or click **<CTRL>+A** to select all text.
   Note: You can choose these settings before you type any text into your document.

2. In the **Paragraph** group in the **Home** tab, click on the **Line Spacing** button.

3. Select one of the preset spacing options available.

4. To choose another option, click **Line Spacing Options** from this menu and then select an option under **Spacing**. The options are:

   - **Single:** Alters the spacing to the largest font used in the line of text and includes a small amount of extra space. The amount of extra space varies depending on the font that is used.

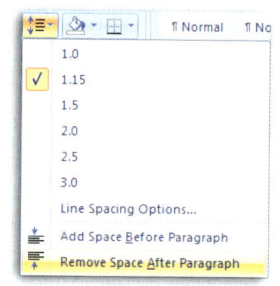

   Joseph and the Turtle

   Once upon a time there was a boy who loved animals. He walked by the local pet shop every morning on his way to school. One morning while he was walking by, he noticed a new animal in the window. It was a turtle larger than the size of his head. He was amazed by what he saw. He stood in the window for a few minutes just watching the turtle. He said to himself, "I think he looks like a nice animal. I think I will stop and see him on my way home from school". And that is just what he did.

QuickClicks: Microsoft Word 2007

format

- **1.5 lines:** One and a half times single line spacing.

- **Double:** Twice the size of single line spacing.

- **At least:** Sets the minimum line spacing that is needed to fit the largest font or graphic in that line of text.

- **Exactly:** Sets fixed line spacing, expressed in font points. For instance, if the text is in a 14-point font, you can specify 20-points as the line spacing.

- **Multiple:** Sets line spacing relative to the current font. For instance, setting line spacing to 3 increases the space by 300%.

Adjust Line and Paragraph Spacing

Adjust Line and Paragraph Spacing (continued)

Adjust Paragraph Spacing

1. Select the paragraph(s) to adjust the paragraph spacing by highlighting the paragraph.

2. In the **Paragraph** group on the **Page Layout** tab, click the arrow next to **Spacing Before** or **Spacing After** and select a preset amount, or type in the amount of space required.

Widows and Orphans

A widow occurs when the last line of a paragraph appears by itself at the top of a new page. An orphan is the first line of a paragraph by itself at the bottom of a page. You can use the Widow/Orphan Control option to automatically keep paragraph text together. If a widow or orphan occurs, Word adjusts the paragraph to make sure at least two lines appear together on the next page.

1. Select the paragraph you want to keep together.

2. Click the **Paragraph** dialog box launcher on the **Home** tab.

3. Click the **Line and Page Breaks** tab.

QuickClicks: Microsoft Word 2007

format

4. Choose an option:

   - **Widow/Orphan control:** Select this check box to avoid paragraphs ending with a single word on a line or a single line at the top of a page **A**.

   - **Keep with next:** Select this check box to group paragraphs together **B**.

   - **Keep lines together:** Select this check box to keep paragraph lines together **C**.

   - **Page break before:** Select this check box to precede a paragraph with a page break **D**.

5. Click **OK** to apply changes **E**.

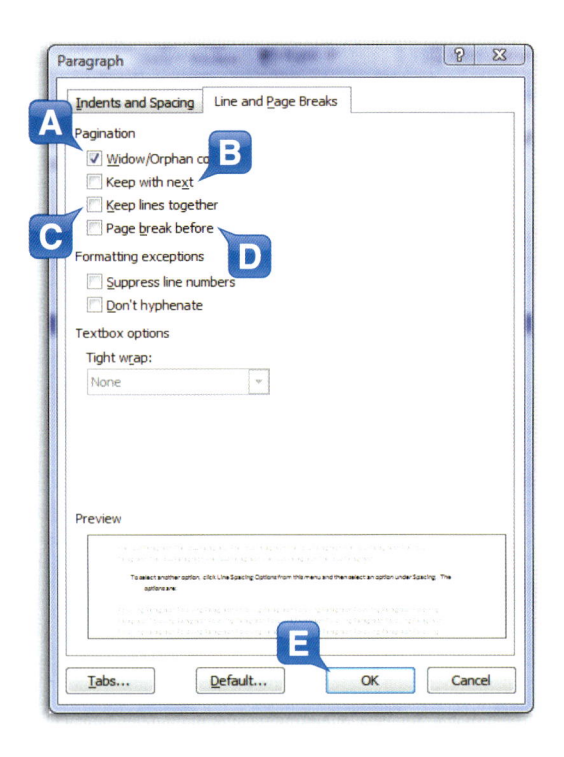

> **Bright Idea:** If you use the same settings repeatedly, create a template with those settings OR a macro to adjust the settings to your standard layout.

> **Caution:** Line and paragraph spacing information is stored "in" the paragraph mark at the end of a line. You must include this paragraph marker ¶ in your selection to be sure your changes apply to the appropriate text. Click the **Paragraph** button in the **Paragraph** group of the **Home** tab to reveal these symbols.

Adjust Line and Paragraph Spacing   **4**

2 Adjust Text Alignment and Tabs

Difficulty: ●○○○

PROBLEM You want to emphasize the title of a document or a portion of a document by centering the text so that the reader's eyes are drawn to it. In addition, you want to line up your text along a margin to make the presentation neat and symmetrical.

SOLUTION Text alignment determines the appearance and orientation of the edges of the paragraph. These options are left-aligned, right-aligned, centered, and justified. These elements can be used for both space and document design purposes.

Tab stops enable you to line up text to the left, right, center, or to a decimal character. You can insert specific characters, such as periods or dashes, before the tabs.

Step-by-Step

Text Alignment

1. Select the text to be aligned.

2. In the **Paragraph** group on the **Home** tab, click the desired alignment for the text from the options:

    - **Align Left**: Aligns all selected text to the left margin.

6   QuickClicks: Microsoft Word 2007

- **Align Right**: Aligns all selected text to the right margin.

  > When attending a baseball game, it's important to remember why people are there. First, there's the game. The pureness of baseball - the balls, the bats; the diamond; the dirt –RBIs and home runs –it's a true miracle for a true baseball fan. Second, there's the experience. The people yelling. The baseball hats. The vulgarity (it happens) and the smell. You know who you are. The smell of the baseball game ...it's something most can only dream of. And lastly, there's the grub. The beer, the peanuts, the cracker jacks and the dogs. Need I say more?

- **Center**: Centers all selected text between the margins.

  > When attending a baseball game, it's important to remember why people are there. First, there's the game. The pureness of baseball - the balls, the bats; the diamond; the dirt –RBIs and home runs –it's a true miracle for a true baseball fan. Second, there's the experience. The people yelling. The baseball hats. The vulgarity (it happens) and the smell. You know who you are. The smell of the baseball game ...it's something most can only dream of. And lastly, there's the grub. The beer, the peanuts, the cracker jacks and the dogs. Need I say more?

- **Justify**: Aligns all selected text evenly along the left and right margins. The last line of text in a paragraph may be shorter than the other lines.

  > When attending a baseball game, it's important to remember why people are there. First, there's the game. The pureness of baseball - the balls, the bats; the diamond; the dirt –RBIs and home runs –it's a true miracle for a true baseball fan. Second, there's the experience. The people yelling. The baseball hats. The vulgarity (it happens) and the smell. You know who you are. The smell of the baseball game ...it's something most can only dream of. And lastly, there's the grub. The beer, the peanuts, the cracker jacks and the dogs. Need I say more?

Adjust Text Alignment and Tabs (continued)

Set Tab Stops

1. Find the horizontal ruler that runs along the top of the document. If you do not see the ruler, click the **View Ruler** button at the top of the vertical scroll bar or click the **Ruler** box in the **Show/Hide** group on the **View** tab **A**.

2. Set tabs by clicking the tab selector at the left end of the ruler to toggle through the tab options until it displays the type of tab you want.

   - **Left Tab Stop**: Sets the start position of text that will run to the right as you type.

   - **Center Tab Stop**: Sets the position of the middle of the text. The text centers on this position as you type.

   - **Right Tab Stop**: Sets the right end of the text. As you type, the text moves to the left.

   - **Decimal Tab Stop**: Aligns numbers around a decimal point. No matter how many numbers are used, the decimal point will stay in the same position. You cannot use the decimal tab to align numbers around any other character.

- **Bar Tab Stop**: This type of tab stop does not position text. When a bar stop is set at a particular position, pressing Tab to move to that spot places a vertical line the same height as that line of text. When several Bar Stops appear in consecutive lines, they form a solid vertical divider line, making the tabbed list resemble a table.

3 | Arrange Text in Columns

Difficulty: ●●●○

PROBLEM You want to create a one-page newsletter. Arranging your text in a normal one-column manner on your page is pushing the text onto a second page. You have enough white space to add columns and make your one-page newsletter look neat and professional.

SOLUTION Columns allow you to divide a page or area of text vertically into two or more sections. The ability to arrange text in columns is particularly useful for newspaper style documents such as newsletters, training materials, and flyers.

Step-by-Step

1. Position the cursor where you would like to insert the columns.

2. On the **Page Layout** tab, in the **Page Setup** group, click the **Columns** button **A**.

3. From the dropdown menu, select the number of columns **B** to insert into the document.

4. Word automatically inserts the columns into your document. 🔥

10 QuickClicks: Microsoft Word 2007

format

Insert a Column Break

You may decide that you would like one column shorter than the other. This can be done easily by inserting a column break.

1. Position your cursor where you would like to insert the column break.

2. On the **Page Layout** tab, in the **Page Setup** group, click the **Breaks** button **C**.

3. From the dropdown menu, select **Column** **D**.

4. Any text typed will begin in the next column. If there is already text following the cursor, it will be moved to the next column.

Arrange Text in Columns

Arrange Text in Columns (continued)

Insert a Continuous Break

You may not want the entire page to contain columns. In that case, insert a continuous break in your document. You can insert one before and one after the section that contains columns. This can add a dramatic effect to your document.

1. Place your cursor where you want the first break.

2. On the **Page Layout** tab, in the **Page Setup** group, click the **Breaks** button.

3. From the dropdown menu, click **Continuous** E.

12   QuickClicks: Microsoft Word 2007

format

Bright Idea: You can apply separate page setup formatting to different sections of your document, such as colors, shading, or borders.

Hot Tip: Microsoft Word 2007, by default, sets all columns to equal width. However, you can edit the spacing of the columns in order to fit the needs of the document by disabling the **Equal Column Width** checkbox and setting your own column widths. On the **Page Layout** tab, in the **Page Setup** group, click **Columns** and select **More Columns**. If you want a vertical line to appear between the columns, select the **Line Between** checkbox. The line is black, fixed width, and cannot be edited.

Arrange Text in Columns

4 Apply Borders and Shading to Text or a Page

Difficulty: ●●○○

PROBLEM You are launching a new dress code policy for your company. To make it more appealing to employees, you want to create a page border and background shading that attract the eye and showcase the images of proper attire on the page. To maintain a consistent artistic style, you want to place a border around the policy and change the color to make it stand out.

SOLUTION **Borders** are lines or graphics that appear around a page, paragraph, selected text, or table cells. With borders, you can change the line style, width, and colors or add special effects, such as shadows and 3D elements. **Shading** is a color that fills the background of selected text, paragraphs, or table cells. Applying border or shading effects is usually done to modify the overall style, design, or presentation of the material.

Step-by-Step

1. Select the text where a border and/or shading is desired. To apply settings to a whole page, click anywhere on the page.

2. On the **Page Layout** tab, in the **Page Background** group, select **Page Borders** **A**.

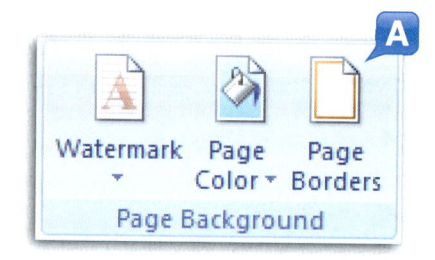

14 QuickClicks: Microsoft Word 2007

format

3. In the **Borders and Shading** dialog box, select a Setting **B**, Style **C**, Color **D**, Width **E**, and/or Art **F**

   a. To apply settings to text only, set options on the **Borders** **G** tab of the dialog box.

   b. To apply settings to the page or document, set options on the **Page Border** **H** tab of the dialog box.

4. Select **Text**, **Paragraph**, or **Whole Document** in the **Apply to** box **I**.

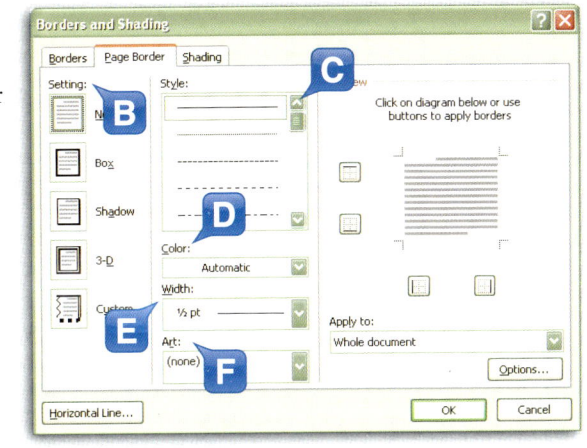

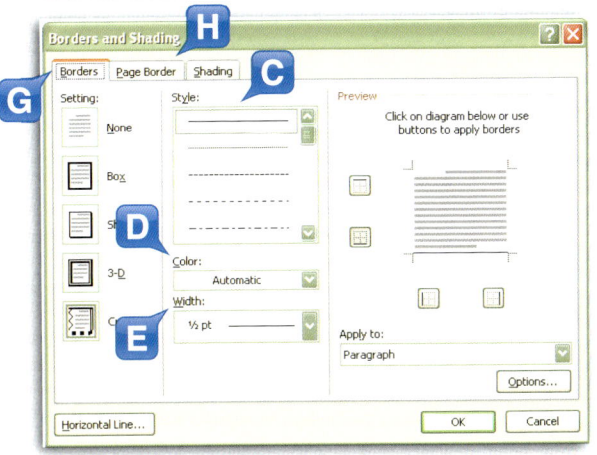

Apply Borders and Shading to Text or a Page   15

Apply Borders and Shading to Text or a Page (continued)

5. Click the **Shading** tab **J** select the fill color and/or patterns to apply.

6. Select **Text**, **Paragraph** or **Whole Document** in the **Apply to** box **I**.

7. Click **OK** to apply the formatting **K**. 🔥

16   QuickClicks: Microsoft Word 2007

format

🔥 **Hot Tip:** If you select text from the beginning of a line to the end of a paragraph and add a border, it will put a box around that whole section, like this.

```
Three Keys to Overcoming Writer's Block

Freewriting
Brainstorming
Mindmapping
```

Apply Borders and Shading to Text or a Page

5 Apply Styles to Text

Difficulty: ●●○○

PROBLEM You are pleased with the content and organization of your document and are ready to make it more visually appealing.

SOLUTION Apply style to your text. Style formatting can be applied to individual characters, words, phrases, paragraphs, whole pages, or documents. Options include font (or typeface, such as Arial or Times New Roman), font style (such as bold or italics), size, color, and effects. Adding style elements can change the entire look of a document. Style selections can enhance or simplify the impact of document elements, such as tables of contents, headings, and lists.

Microsoft Word provides predesigned Quick Styles for easy selection. These sets include a Normal style for body text and a variety of styles for lists, quotes, references, and text that you want to emphasize or highlight within the document. Most style changes are made for design and usability purposes and are very simple to apply.

See Appendix C–Formatting Options; Create a Table of Contents; Create a PowerPoint Presentation From a Word Document; Create a Document Summary

Step-by-Step

Apply a Quick Style

1. Select the text you want to format.

2. On the **Home** tab, in the **Styles** group, click the **More** dropdown arrow **A** to scroll through the list of Quick Styles.

3. Click the style to apply to your text.

format

Changing a Style Set

1. On the **Home** tab, in the **Styles** group, click the **Change Styles** button **B**.

2. Select **Style Set** **C** and click the style set to apply **D**.

Create a Style Set

1. Format a document with the style that you want to save.

2. On the **Home** tab, in the **Styles** group, click the **Change Styles** button **B**.

3. Select **Style Set** **C**.

4. Click **Save as Quick Style Set** **E**.

5. In the **Save Quick Style Set** dialog box, type a file name **F**.

6. Click **Save** **G**. 🔥

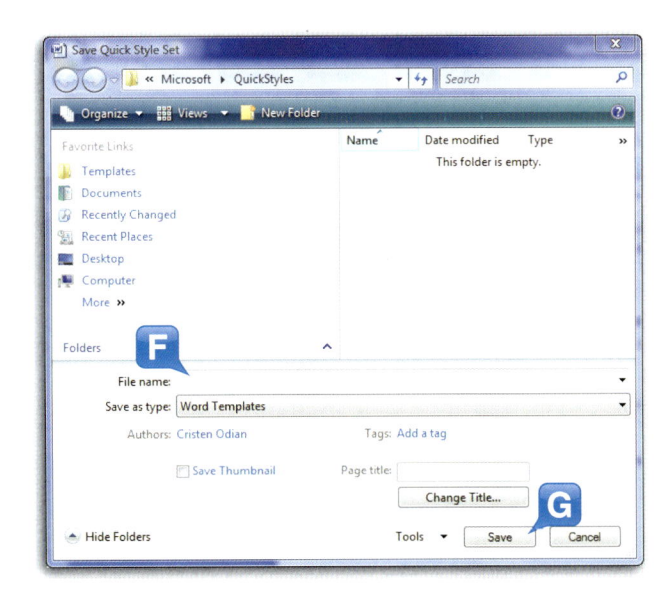

Apply Styles to Text   19

5 Apply Styles to Text (continued)

Create a New Style

Word provides a variety of styles to choose from. However, sometimes you need to create a new style or modify an existing one to get exactly the appearance you want. You can create a paragraph or character style. A paragraph style is a group of format settings applied to all of the text within a paragraph. A character style is a group of format settings applied to any block of text that a user selects.

1. Select the text with the formatting you want to save.

2. On the **Home** tab, click the **More** dropdown arrow and select **Save Selection as a New Quick Style**.

3. Type a short, descriptive name for the new style.

4. Click **Modify**.

20   QuickClicks: Microsoft Word 2007

format

5. Click the **Style type** K dropdown arrow and click:

   - **Paragraph** to include the selected text's line spacing and margins in the style.

   - **Character** to include only formatting, such as font, size, and italics, in the style.

   - **Linked** to include both paragraph and character style.

6. Click the **Style for following paragraph** L dropdown arrow and click the name of the style you want to apply after a paragraph with the new style.

7. In the **Formatting** M section, select the formatting options you want.

8. To add the style to the **Quick Style Gallery**, select the **Add to Quick Style** N list check box.

9. Click **OK** O.

> **Quickest Click:** Apply a style quickly by using the **Format Painter**. Select the text with the format you want to copy. Click the **Format Painter** button and then select the text where you want to copy the format. The newly highlighted text will automatically be formatted.

> **Hot Tip:** You can save your Style Set as a template by changing the **Save as type** to Word Template in the **Save Quick Style Set** dialog box.

Apply Styles to Text   21

6 Insert a Numbered or Bulleted List

Difficulty: ●○○○

PROBLEM You are making a list that will sit amidst paragraphs of text. You want to make the list stand out from the rest of the text, making it easier to work with and read.

SOLUTION Use a numbered or bulleted list. Lists help break text into manageable chunks.

Step-by-Step

There are two ways to approach creating a list. First you can type the entire list, select all the text and then click the **Bullets** A or **Numbering** B button. Second, you can click one of the list buttons first and then type. Each time you press **Enter**, a new bullet or number is created. Pressing **Enter** at a blank bullet or number returns you to regular formatting.

1. Place cursor in the position where your list should begin.

2. On the **Home** tab, in the **Paragraph** group, click the **Bullets** A or the **Numbering** B button. 💡

3. The first bullet or number character will appear in the document.

4. To edit the format/style of the bullet or number character, click the arrow on the right side of the button to view and select options.

Normal List	Bulleted List	Numbered List
Item One Item Two Item Three Item Four	• Item One • Item Two • Item Three • Item Four	1. Item One 2. Item Two 3. Item Three 4. Item Four

format

Change Bullet or Number Styles

1. Select the list and click the **Home** tab.

2. Click the **Bullets** or **Numbering** button arrow.

3. Select a predefined format or click **Define New Bullet** or **Define New Number Format**.

4. To add a graphic bullet, click **Symbol** or **Picture** and select an image.

5. Specify the font style/size and alignment.

6. Click **OK** to apply changes.

Bulleted List Using Symbols	Bulleted List Using Pictures
∞ Item One ∞ Item Two ∞ Item Three ∞ Item Four	● Item One ● Item Two ● Item Three ● Item Four

CONTINUE

Insert a Numbered or Bulleted List   23

Insert a Numbered or Bulleted List (continued)

Create a Multi-Level Bulleted or Numbered List/Outline

1. Begin typing your list using either bullets or numbers.

2. At the position you want to indent to the next level, press **Tab**.

3. Type your text and press **Enter**. 🔥

4. Press **Shift+Tab** to return to the previous level bullet or number. ⚠️

Multi-Level Bulleted List

• Item One
    o Item One–A
    o Item One–B
• Item Two
    o Item Two–A
    o Item Two–B

Multi-Level Numbered List

1. Item One
    a. Item One–A
    b. Item One–B
2. Item Two
    a. Item Two–A
    b. Item Two–B

format

Quickest Click: To return to the previous level in your list for the next item, click **Enter** multiple times until you go back to the desired level.

Hot Tip: To format the list type, select the list, click the **Multi-Level List** button on the **Home** tab and select a format.

Bright Idea: Quickly create a numbered list by following these easy steps:
1. Place your cursor where you want to begin the list.
2. Type "**1**."
3. Click the **Spacebar** and enter your text.
4. Press **Enter** to continue the numbering.
5. Press **Enter** and **Backspace** to end the list.

Caution: If you are creating a list in a Table, use the **Increase Indent** button in the **Paragraph** group on the **Home** tab to create the next level in your list or the **Decrease Indent** button to return to the previous level.

Insert a Numbered or Bulleted List 25

7 Apply a Consistent Look and Feel to a Document

Difficulty: ●●○○

PROBLEM You are satisfied with the content of your document, but you want to apply a coordinated color palette to create a professional and polished finish.

SOLUTION Use a preset or custom "theme." Themes are made up of colors, fonts, graphics, and effects that help you add a coordinated element of design to your documents. You can quickly format an entire document (or even a set of documents) by applying a theme. Microsoft Word 2007 comes with a variety of predesigned themes to choose from.

See Also: Create a Custom Look and Feel to Use in Documents

Step-by-Step

View and Apply a Theme

1. Open the document you want to edit.

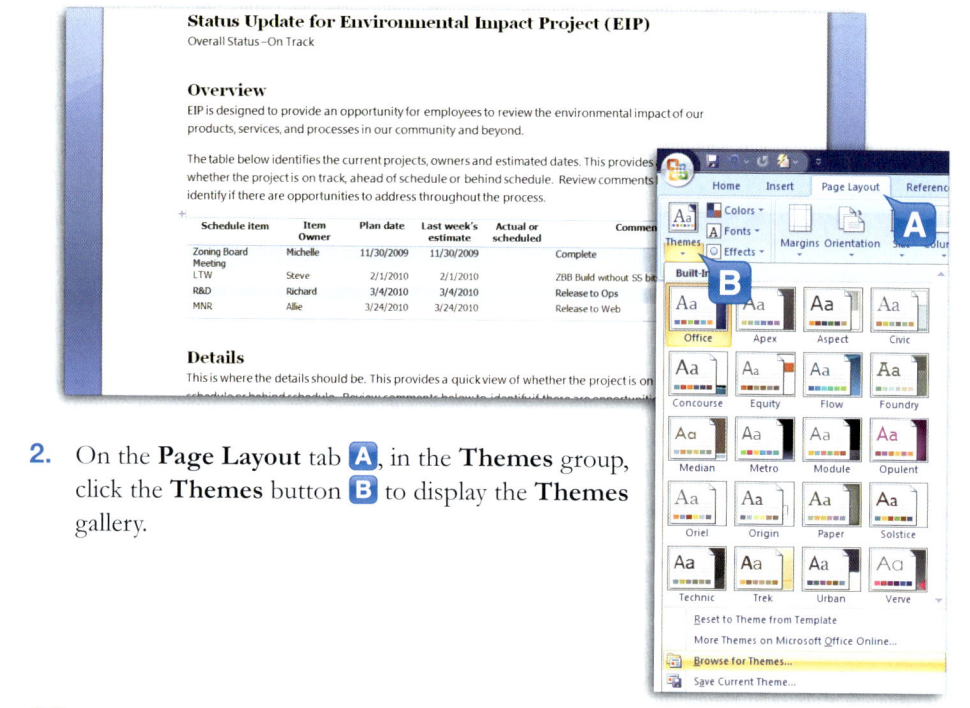

2. On the **Page Layout** tab **A**, in the **Themes** group, click the **Themes** button **B** to display the **Themes** gallery.

26   QuickClicks: Microsoft Word 2007

format

3. Point to a theme. A live preview of the theme appears in the document.

4. Click the theme you want to apply.

Bright Idea: If you do not find a theme you want in the **Themes** gallery, you can search the Microsoft Office Online web site to download and use online themes. Click the **Page Layout** tab, click the **Themes** button, and then click **More Themes on Microsoft Office Online**.

Apply a Consistent Look and Feel to a Document   27

8 Create a Custom Look and Feel to Use in Documents

Difficulty: ●●○○

PROBLEM Your marketing team has launched a new branding campaign for your organization. All of the colors, images, and fonts have changed to project a more modern image. You must create a new look and feel for all documentation to match the new branding scheme.

SOLUTION Create a custom theme. Using a pre-set theme is fast and easy, but a custom theme provides some additional benefits. A custom theme allows you to incorporate your organization's colors, fonts, graphics, and style into your document's appearance. You can either create a theme from scratch, or you can modify an existing theme.

See Also: Apply a Consistent Look and Feel to a Document

> **What Microsoft Calls It:** Theme or Document Theme

Step-by-Step

Create Color Set

There are 12 placeholders, including text/background, accent, and hyperlinks. Each placeholder needs to be assigned a certain color.

1. On the **Page Layout** A tab, in the **Themes** B group, open the theme **Colors** C menu

2. Choose **Create New Theme Colors** D.

28   QuickClicks: Microsoft Word 2007

format

3. Click one of the colors **E** or select **More Colors** **F** to select an alternate color.

4. Repeat this step for all placeholders.

5. In the **Name** box **G**, type a name for the color scheme.

6. Click **Save** to create new color set **H**.

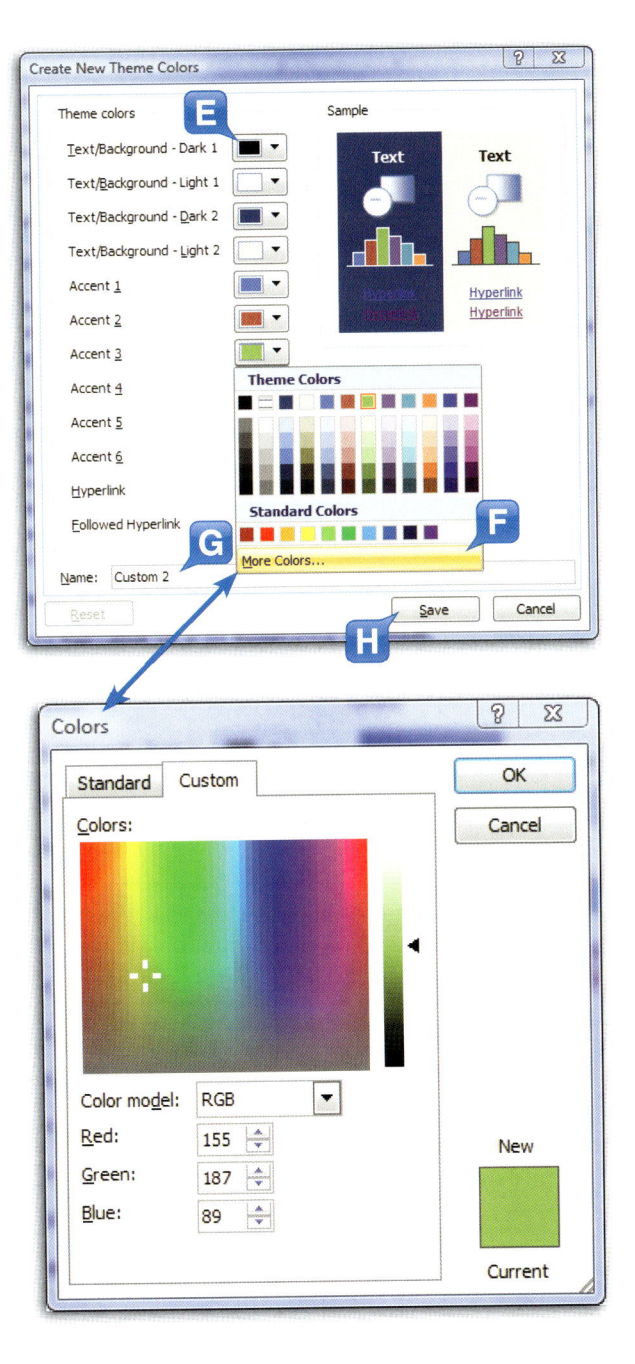

Create a Custom Look and Feel to Use in Documents   29

8 Create Custom Look and Feel to Use in Documents (continued)

Create Font Set

1. On the **Page Layout** tab, in the **Themes** group, select **Fonts**.

2. Select **Create New Theme Fonts** **I**.

3. In the **Create New Theme Fonts** dialog box, use the dropdown menu to select **Heading** and **Body** fonts **J**.

4. In the **Name** box **K**, type a name for the new font set.

5. Click **Save** to create new font set **L**.

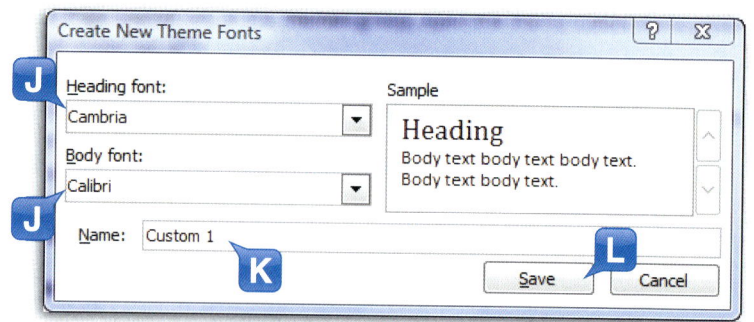

format

Choose and Apply a Custom Theme

1. On the **Page Layout** tab, in the **Themes** group, click the **Themes** button **M**.

2. Click **Browse for Themes** **N**.

3. If you want to open a specific file type, click the **Files of Type** dropdown arrow **O**, and then select **Office Theme** file type.

4. If your file is located in another folder, browse to locate the folder.

5. Click the theme file you want and click **Open** **P**.

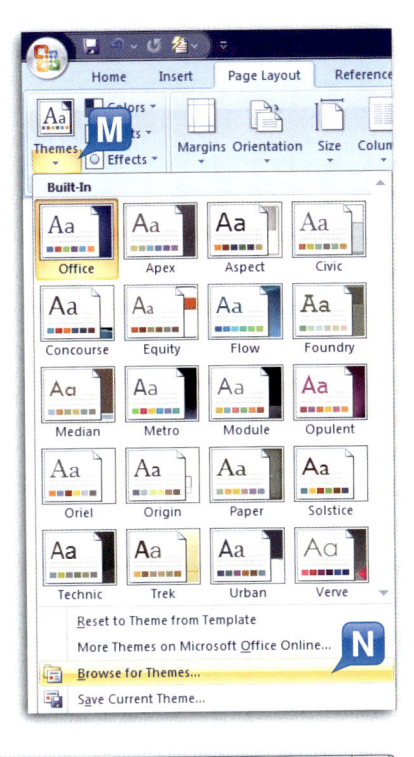

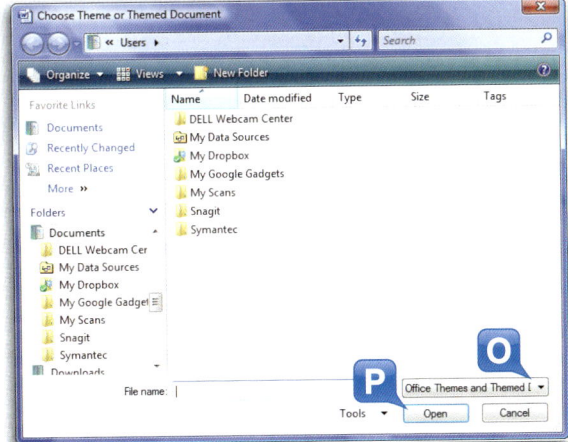

Create a Custom Look and Feel to Use in Documents   31

9 | Apply a Watermark to a Page

Difficulty: ●○○○

PROBLEM You create a draft of a document and want to send it out for review. However, you want to make it clear to readers that this is a draft and not a final version.

SOLUTION A watermark is text that appears behind the main body of a document in the form of a grayed-out image. In Microsoft Word 2007, you can select from several pre-set watermarks or create a watermark using custom text. Watermarks are typically used to mark documents as CONFIDENTIAL or DRAFT. However, watermarks can consist of symbols (© ™ ®), company names, or even images.

Step-by-Step

1. On the **Page Layout** tab, in the **Page Background** group, click the **Watermark** button **A**.

2. In the menu, scroll down to select a pre-formatted watermark.

3. To create a custom watermark, click **Custom Watermark** from the dialog box menu **B**.

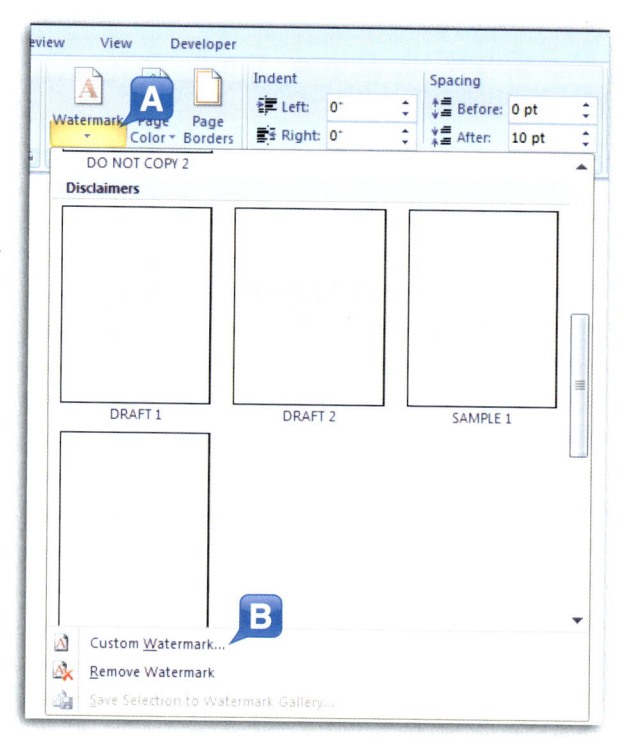

32   QuickClicks: Microsoft Word 2007

format

4. In the **Printed Watermark** dialog box C, select from the following options:

   a. **No watermark** D: This option removes any watermark images or text from the document.

Apply a Watermark to a Page   33

9 Apply a Watermark to a Page (continued)

b. **Picture watermark** E:
This option places a picture behind the main document in a washed-out format so it doesn't obstruct the main text of the document. Select the location of the picture and specify the size. If you do not want the picture washed-out, uncheck the **Washout** check box F.

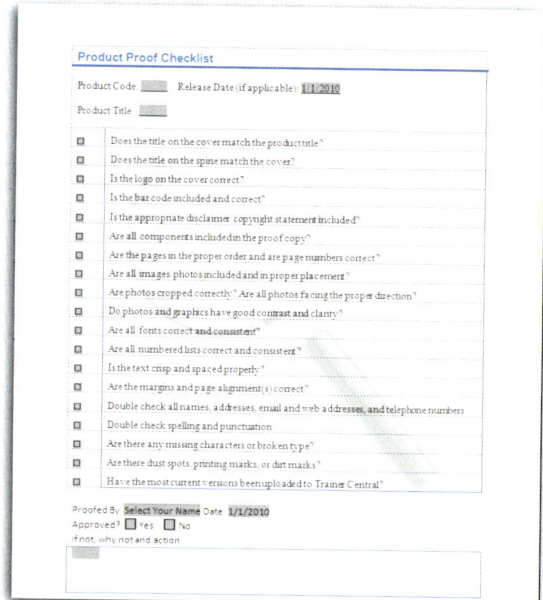

34   QuickClicks: Microsoft Word 2007

format

c. **Text watermark** G: This option places any text you enter as a watermark. Select the language, text, font, size, color, and layout of the text.

5. Click **OK** H to apply changes and return to document.

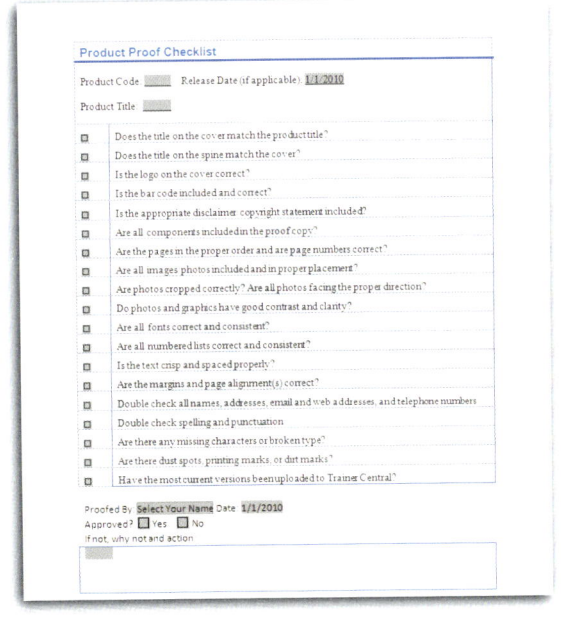

Apply a Watermark to a Page   35

10 Insert and Customize WordArt

Difficulty: ●○○○

PROBLEM You are creating a Yard Sale flyer to send out to your neighborhood. You want the words "Yard Sale" to have an artistic look and draw attention.

SOLUTION WordArt is an object that combines graphic elements with text. WordArt is useful when you need to create quick and artistic ways of displaying company names, headings, graphics for flyers, or newsletter headings.

Step-by-Step

Creating WordArt Text

1. On the **Insert** tab, in the **Text** group, click the **WordArt** button **A** and click one of the **WordArt** styles **B**.

2. In the **WordArt** text box **C**, type the text you want.

3. Use the **Font** **D** options to modify the text you entered.

4. Click **OK** **E** to finish.

36 QuickClicks: Microsoft Word 2007

illustrate

Format WordArt Text

1. Double-click the **WordArt** object you want to edit.

2. Click the **Format** tab under **WordArt** Tools.

3. Select a style from the list or click **More** and select a style to preview.

4. Click the style you want from the gallery to apply.

> **Hot Tip:** You can convert text in a text box to **WordArt**. Click the **Insert** tab, click the **WordArt** button, and then click the **WordArt** text style you want to apply.

Insert and Customize WordArt   37

11 Insert a Picture or Piece of Clip Art

Difficulty: ●○○○

PROBLEM You want to place images into your document that will enhance the content and presentation of your Word project.

SOLUTION Graphics are used to enhance design and to support text in documents. There are two ways to insert graphic images. The first is to insert a picture from an image file available to the user. The second is to insert Clip Art, which is a gallery of ready-made pieces of graphic art, such as illustrations, borders, or backgrounds. The Clip Art gallery is organized by keyword. Once a graphic is placed into a document, it can be formatted so that it fits with your text and other document elements.

See Also: Tip – Edit an Image's Appearance and Tip – Group and Stack Images

Step-by-Step

Insert an Image

1. Position the cursor where the image should be placed.

2. On the **Insert** tab, in the **Illustrations** group, select **Picture** or **Clip Art**, depending upon the location of the graphic.

    a. In the **Picture** dialog box, browse to select the location of your image, and click **OK** to insert into the document.

    b. In the **Clip Art** gallery, type a keyword to view the **Clip Art** images available to choose from. Once you have chosen an image, click on it to insert it into the document.

illustrate

Text Wrapping

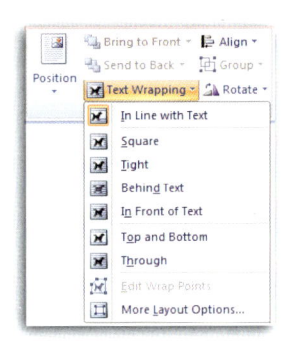

The image may push your text around the page in a disruptive way. To edit text wrapping in relation to the image:

1. Click the **Text Wrapping** button in the **Arrange** group on the **Picture Tools Format** tab.

2. Select the Wrapping Style
   - **In Line with Text** 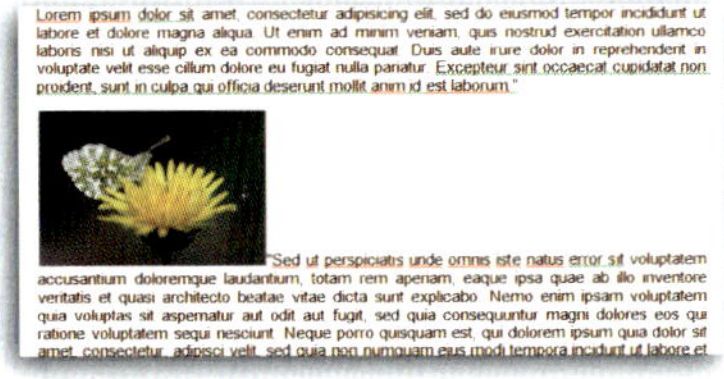
   - **Square** 
   - **Tight** 
   - **Behind Text** 
   - **In Front of Text** 
   - **Top and Bottom** 
   - **Through** 
   - **More Layout Options**–provides additional options.

Insert a Picture or Piece of Clip Art   39

11 Insert a Picture or Piece of Clip Art (continued)

Crop, Resize, or Rotate the Image

- To resize an image–right-click the image and select **Size** from the menu.

In the **Size** dialog box, edit the size (height and width) **A**, rotation (0-360 degrees) **B**, or scale **C** of the image.

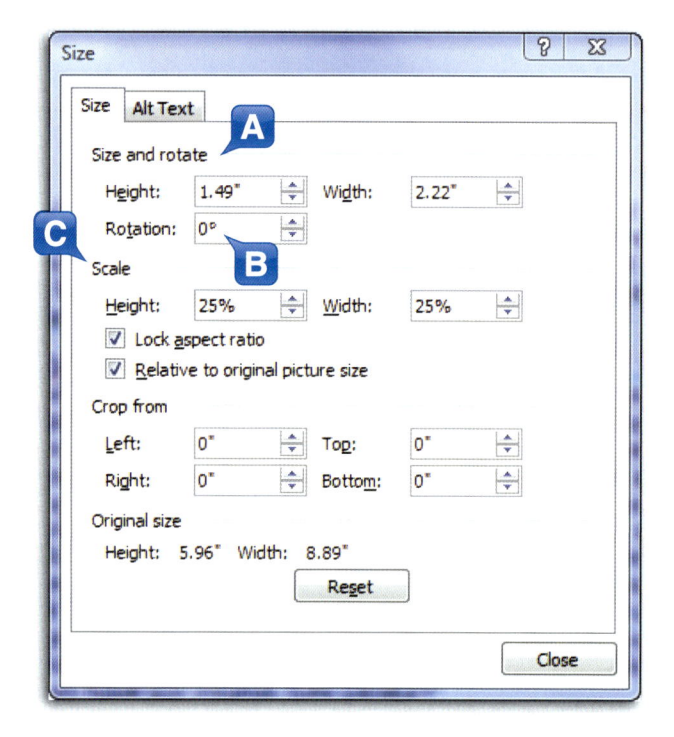

illustrate

- To crop the image–first click on it, then select the **Crop** button **D** in the **Size** group on the **Format** tab. Click and drag the black line "handles" **E** at the corners and on each side of the image to trim unneeded pieces.
- To rotate the image–select it and then click the **Rotate** button **F** in the **Arrange** group on the **Format** tab. Choose a rotation direction or flip option from the dropdown menu **G**.

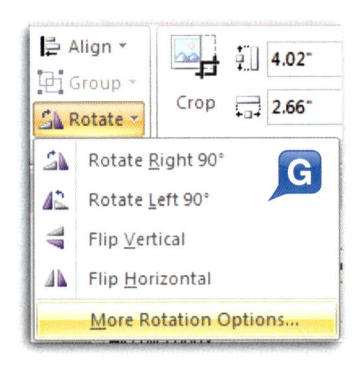

Quickest Click: Right-click on the image, select **Text Wrapping**, and select the wrapping style.

Hot Tip: Keep in mind the importance of utilizing solid design principles when including graphic elements into documents. A picture should add to, not detract from, the message. Principles of balance, symmetry, and color, for example, should be considered.

Bright Idea: Shrink your document's file size by compressing images and removing cropped area data. To compress images in your document, select any image and then click the **Compress Pictures** button in the **Adjust** group on the **Format** tab. You may apply compression to just the selected image or to all images in the document.

Insert a Picture or Piece of Clip Art   41

12 Edit an Image's Appearance

Difficulty: ●○○○

PROBLEM You want to put an image of a house into your document to support the content. You have a great image, but the color clashes with the rest of the images in the document.

SOLUTION Word 2007 includes several robust image editing tools, including those that allow you to make changes to an image's color, transparency, brightness, contrast and more. Graphics are used to enhance the design and to support the text in documents. There are two ways to insert graphic images. The first is to insert a picture from an image file available to the user. The second is to insert Clip Art, which is a gallery of ready-made pieces of graphic art, such as illustrations, borders, or backgrounds. The Clip Art gallery is organized by keyword. Once a graphic is placed into a document, it can be formatted so that it fits with your text and other document elements.

See Also: Tip–Insert a Picture or Clip Art; Stack and Group Images in a Document

Step-by-Step

Adjust Image Color

1. Double-click the image to bring up the **Picture Tools Format** tab.

2. In the **Adjust** group, select the **Recolor** button.

3. Scroll over the menu options to preview the color scheme applied to the image.
   - **Automatic**: displays original coloring.
   - **Grayscale**: converts colors into whites, blacks, and shades of gray.

42   QuickClicks: Microsoft Word 2007

- **Black and White**: converts colors into black and white only.
- **Washout**: converts colors into whites and very light colors.

4. Select a color scheme from the menu or select **More Variations** and choose a different theme color.

Set Transparent Color

1. Double-click the image to bring up the **Picture Tools Format** tab.
2. In the **Adjust** group, select the **Recolor** button.
3. Select **Set Transparent Color**.
4. The mouse pointer turns into a pen.
5. Click the background of the picture (or another area to make transparent).
6. All instances of that color become transparent.

Edit an Image's Appearance

12 Edit an Image's Appearance (continued)

Change Image Style

1. To add alternate artistic elements to the image, such as 3D rotation or a shadow, right-click the image and select **Format Picture** from the menu.

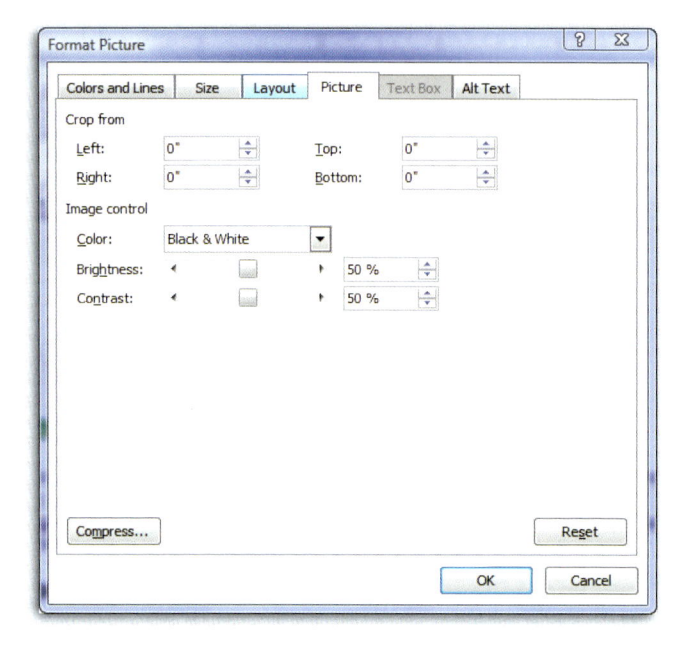

2. Select the element to add to the image, and complete the fields as desired.

   - **Line Color**–Adds a line around the image. You can specify the line's color and style.

   - **Line Style**–Specify the width and style of the line around the image.

44   QuickClicks: Microsoft Word 2007

illustrate

- **Shadow**–Adds a shadow effect to your image.

- **3-D Format**–Adds 3-dimensional formatting to your image.

- **3-D Rotation**–Adds a 3-dimensional rotation to your image.

3. Once edits are made, click **OK** to apply.

> **Hot Tip:** If the picture you are using has a lot of variation of color (such as a photograph of the sunset), this option will not be as useful. The transparency tool is most useful in an image with solid color backgrounds.

> **Caution:** Print a test page or test the image quality in its final format to be certain the changes perform as anticipated. For example, if the edited image looked good in color, but will be printed in black & white, it should be reviewed before finalizing.

Edit an Image's Appearance

13 Stack and Group Images in a Document

Difficulty: ●○○○

PROBLEM You want to create images that overlap one another.

SOLUTION Multiple objects in a document appear in a stacking order, like layers of transparent paper. Stacking is the placement of objects one on top of another. The first object that you draw is on the bottom, and the last object is on the top. You can change the order of these objects by using layering commands. When creating an object consisting of multiple individual shapes, editing those individually can be challenging. Objects can be grouped, ungrouped, or grouped again to make editing easier.

Stack objects on top of one another when you want to create overlapping shapes, add text to an image, or use arrows to point to specific areas in a graphic. You can also move graphics in front of or behind the text layer, like a Watermark, for example.

See Also: Apply a Watermark to a Page; Edit an Image's Appearance; Insert Image or Clip Art

> **What Microsoft Calls It:** Layering and Grouping, Text Wrapping, Bring To Front, Send to Back

Step-by-Step

Layer Items

If you intend to layer items, you must first make sure that **In Line with Text** is not selected as the image's **Text Wrapping** option. To make sure any selection except **In Line with Text** is chosen, click the image to select it, and then click the **Text Wrapping** button in the **Arrange Group** on the **Format** tab.

1. Select the object to layer.

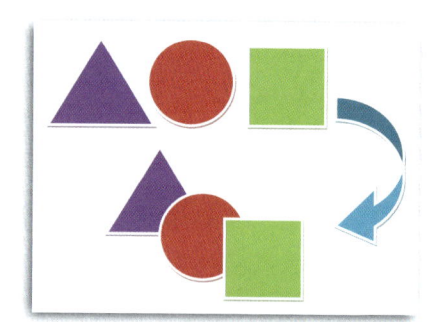

illustrate

2. On the **Page Layout** tab, in the **Arrange** group, click **Bring to Front** **A** or **Send to Back** **B**. By default, graphics are stacked in the order they are drawn.

3. To move an object one position within the layers, open the dropdown in the **Bring to Front** or **Send to Back** **C**.

4. Click either **Bring Forward** or **Send Backward**.

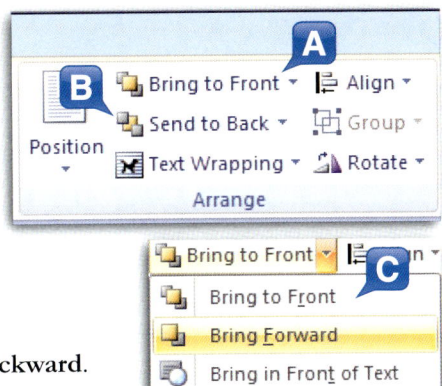

Group Shapes

If you intend to group items, you must first make sure that **In Line with Text** is not selected as the image's **Text Wrapping** option. To make sure any selection except **In Line with Text** is chosen, click the image to select it, and then click the **Text Wrapping** button in the **Arrange Group** on the **Format** tab.

1. Create a grouping by selecting all the pieces (click and drag a box around the entire collection of shapes or click one item, and then hold the **CTRL** key as you click each additional item to add it to the selection).

2. Click the **Format** tab under **Drawing** or **Text Box Tools**.

3. Click the **Group** button.

4. Click **Group**.

5. Individual selection handles disappear and a single set of selection handles appears for the whole group.

Stack and Group Images in a Document   47

13 Stack and Group Images in a Document (continued)

Ungroup Shapes

1. Select the grouped object you want to ungroup.

2. Click the **Format** tab under **Drawing** or **Text Box Tools**.

3. Click the **Group** button.

4. Click **Ungroup**.

Regroup Shapes

1. Select one of the objects in the group you want to regroup.

2. Click the **Format** tab under **Drawing** or **Text Box Tools**.

3. Click the **Group** button.

4. Click **Regroup**.

illustrate

Caution: Some items will not easily group together. If you find your objects will not group, you need to place them on a Drawing Canvas. To create a Drawing Canvas, click the **Shapes** button in the **Illustration** group on the **Insert** tab and select **New Drawing Canvas**. This will insert a bordered frame. Cut and paste each item—one at a time—from its current location to the drawing canvas. Once the objects are on the canvas, you should be able to group them.

Quickest Click: To group shapes, right-click the group, select **Grouping** and then **Group**.

Stack and Group Images in a Document

14 Create a List of All Illustrations in a Document

Difficulty: ●○○○

PROBLEM You created a technical product guide for one of your best-selling products. The product guide contains a large number of images, charts, and figures. Your customers have mentioned that it would help to have a way to quickly scan through the diagrams to find the one they are looking for, instead of flipping through pages.

SOLUTION Create a Table of Figures. A Table of Figures is similar to a Table of Contents, but it indexes diagrams and captions instead of headings. This is useful in documents like technical manuals or scientific reports that include a large number of figures or diagrams. The table can be positioned after the Table of Contents, allowing reviewers easy access to a list of illustrations.

See Also: Insert a Picture or Piece of Clip Art; Edit an Image's Appearance; Stack and Group Images in a Document; Create a Table of Contents

> **What Microsoft Calls It:** Insert a Table of Figures

Step-by-Step

Create Captions

Captions are helpful not only to connect images with your content, but also to provide more information about the illustration. Adding captions to images is also the first step in creating a Table of Figures.

1. Right-click a graphic.
2. Choose **Insert Caption.**
3. In the **Caption** dialog box, type a descriptive caption. The numbering is pre-filled.

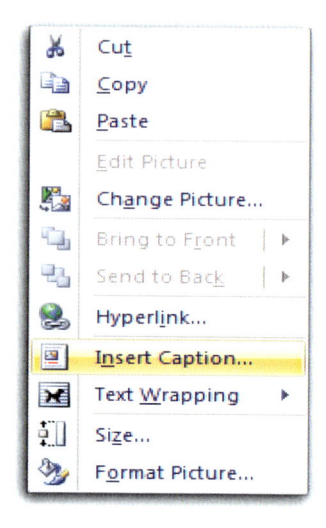

illustrate

4. Select the position where you want the caption to appear—above or below the image.

5. Click **OK** to apply the caption.

6. Repeat these steps for all the images you want in the Table of Figures.

Create a Table of Figures

1. Place your cursor where you want to insert a Table of Figures.

2. On the **References** tab in the **Captions** group, click **Insert Table of Figures** **A**.

3. Click the **Tab Leader** list **B** and select the tab leader (pattern of dots between the entry and the page number) you want to use.

4. Click the **Formats** list **C** and select the format you want for the **Table of Figures**.

5. In the **Options** dialog box, open the **Style** dropdown menu and select **Caption** **D**.

6. Click **OK** **E**.

7. Click **OK** to insert Table of Figures into document.

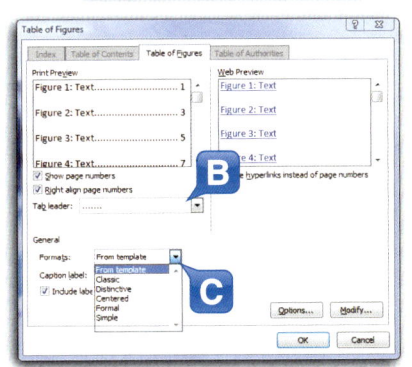

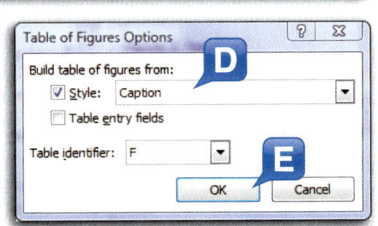

Create a List of All Illustrations in a Document   51

15 Insert Text Box

Difficulty: ●○○○

PROBLEM As an account manager for a small boutique, you have been asked to create a one-page flyer promoting a new product. Instead of spending the money to hire someone with experienced graphics credentials for such a simple project, you would like to do it yourself.

SOLUTION A text box is a shape designed to place text in a document without interacting with standard page margins. Text boxes are especially useful when adding text to a graphic image. However, text boxes are frequently used to enhance the design of professional documents.

Microsoft 2007 offers 36 different standard text box options that vary in style, size, and format. Depending upon the application of a text box, you can either select one of these available presets, or design a custom text box by drawing and formatting the elements. Text can be added to virtually any shape inserted via the Shapes button in the Illustrations group on the Insert tab, whether they are specialized for that purpose (such as thought bubbles and call-outs) or basic figures like squares, cylinders, and stars.

See Also: Stack and Group Images in a Document; Insert and Manage Stored Document Components

Step-by-Step

1. On the **Insert** tab in the **Text** group, click **Text Box** **A**.

2. Several standard text box samples are available to preview and select in the **Text Box** menu **B** or select the option to **Draw Text Box** **C**.

   - The standard options will place a text box template into the document. You should replace default text with your own.

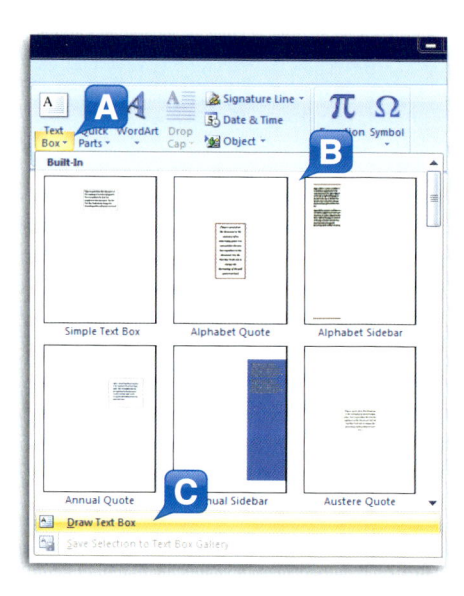

52   QuickClicks: Microsoft Word 2007

design

- Drawing a custom text box allows you to customize the formatting elements of the text box, such as size, font, colors, and borders and shading. 🔥

3. The text box may be moved anywhere in the document by clicking and dragging (or copying/cutting and pasting) it to the preferred location.

Format the Text Box

Place your cursor in the text box. The **Text Box Tools Format** menu D opens on the main ribbon. By selecting the elements in this ribbon, you can reformat the following elements of your text box:

- Text
- Text Box Style
- Shadow and 3-D Effects
- Text Box Arrangement
- Size

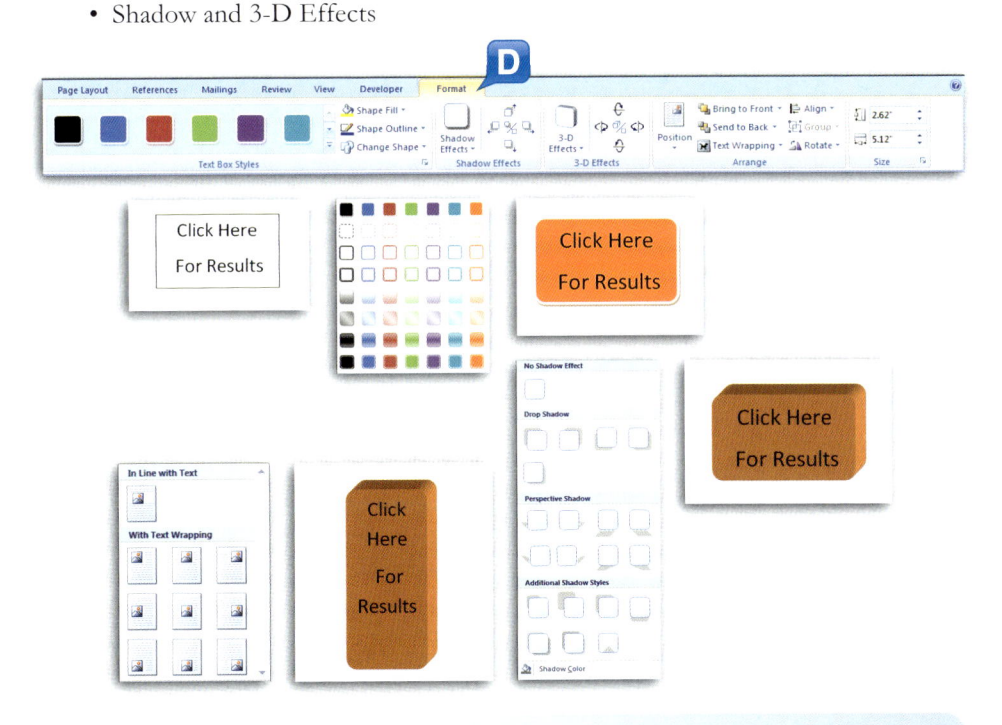

🔥 **Hot Tip:** You can group text boxes and images together.

Insert Text Box   53

16 Add a Table to a Document

Difficulty: ●●●○

PROBLEM You need to categorize the results from a recent wellness survey. You want to organize the data by team and topic. Create a table to organize this data within the rest of your report.

SOLUTION Tables are useful objects, consisting of columns and rows that help organize information in a logical and easy to view format. You can insert a preformatted table that includes sample data, or you can manually choose the number of rows and columns you need. Once created, you can adjust cells, insert or delete rows, columns, and cells, change the alignment of text, sort data, or apply borders and shading.

See Also: Format Table Borders, Layout, and Shading; Import Data from an Excel Spreadsheet into a Document; Perform Calculations in a Table

Step-by-Step

1. Place the cursor where the table should be inserted into the document.

2. On the **Insert** tab, in the **Tables** group, click **Table** **A**.

3. Click **Insert Table** **B**.

4. Under **Table size**, enter the number of columns and rows **C**.

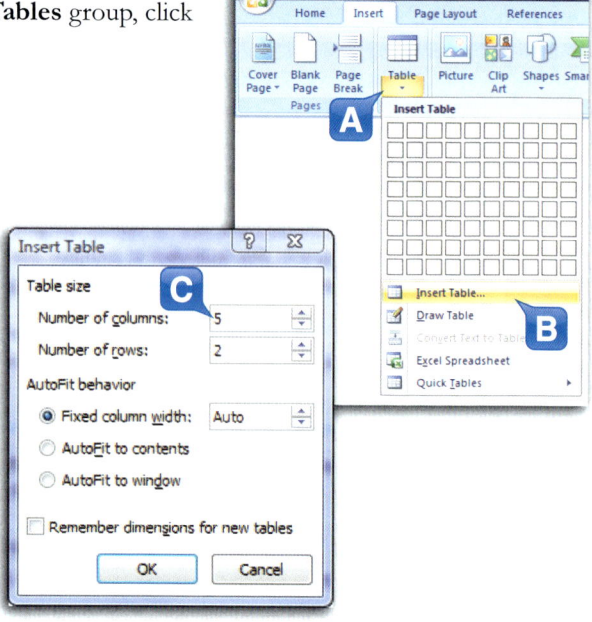

54   QuickClicks: Microsoft Word 2007

design

5. Under **AutoFit behavior**, choose options to adjust the table size.

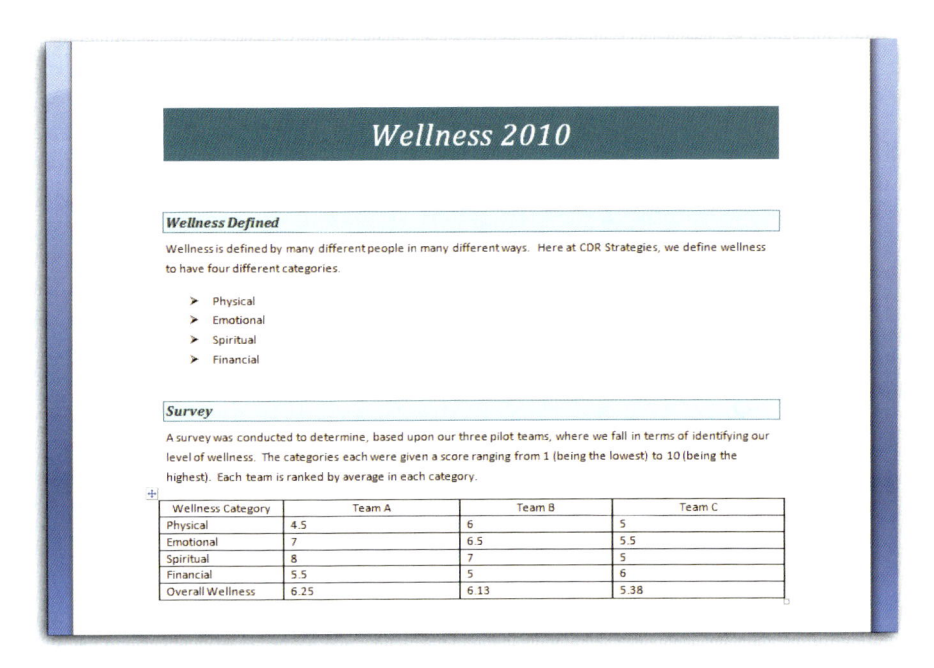

> **Quickest Click:** On the **Insert** tab, in the **Tables** group, click **Table** and drag the mouse to select the number of columns and rows for the table **C**. You can then format the size of the table by selecting the table in your document, then right-click and select **Table Properties**.

> **Bright Idea:** Use a preformatted table to create a quick table by selecting a template from the **Quick Tables** menu, in the **Tables** group on the **Insert** tab. Simply replace the data in the template with your information.

> **Hot Tip:** You can convert text to a table with a few clicks by inserting separator characters, such as commas, to indicate where the text should separate into columns. Use paragraph marks to indicate a new row. Select the text to convert. On the **Insert** tab, in the **Tables** group, click **Table**. Click **Convert Text to Table**. In the dialog box, click the option for the separator character you used.

Add a Table to a Document   55

17 Format Table Borders, Layout, and Shading

Difficulty: ●●○○

PROBLEM You want to highlight every other row of your table to make the information easier to read.

SOLUTION After you create a table, there are multiple options to format the table's borders, layout, and shading. These features enhance the table's design, usability, and function within the document.

See Also: Add a Table to a Document

Step-by-Step

Format Layout

Once a generic table is built, there are a number of modifications that can be applied to the layout of that table. For example, you can add or delete rows and/or columns of the table. You can edit the size of the rows, columns, and cells, and can merge cells together or split one cell into multiple cells.

	Top Three Teams in the League		
	The Cougars	The Colts	The Chargers
Game 1	W	L	W
Game 2	W	W	L
Game 3	L	W	W
Game 4	L	W	L
Game 5	W	L	W
Game 6	W	W	W

After selecting a portion of the table to modify:

Modify Row, Column, and Cell Height and Width

1. Right-click anywhere in the table to select **Table Properties** from the menu.

design

2. The dialog box opens with four tabs, allowing specific modifications such as:

- **Table**: This tab allows you to modify the size (width) of table rows and columns, set the alignment, and to define text wrapping preferences within the table.

- **Row**: This tab allows you to modify the size (height) of a row and define settings such as whether to allow rows to break across pages, and if row information should be repeated at the top of each document page. This is typically done with a table that runs multiple pages and has a single header row at the top.

- **Column**: This tab allows you to modify the size (width) of a column.

- **Cell**: This tab allows you to modify the size of a specific cell, as well as its vertical alignment. If you have defined overall table size properties, you would only specify different information in this tab to create alternate formatting for a specific highlighted cell.

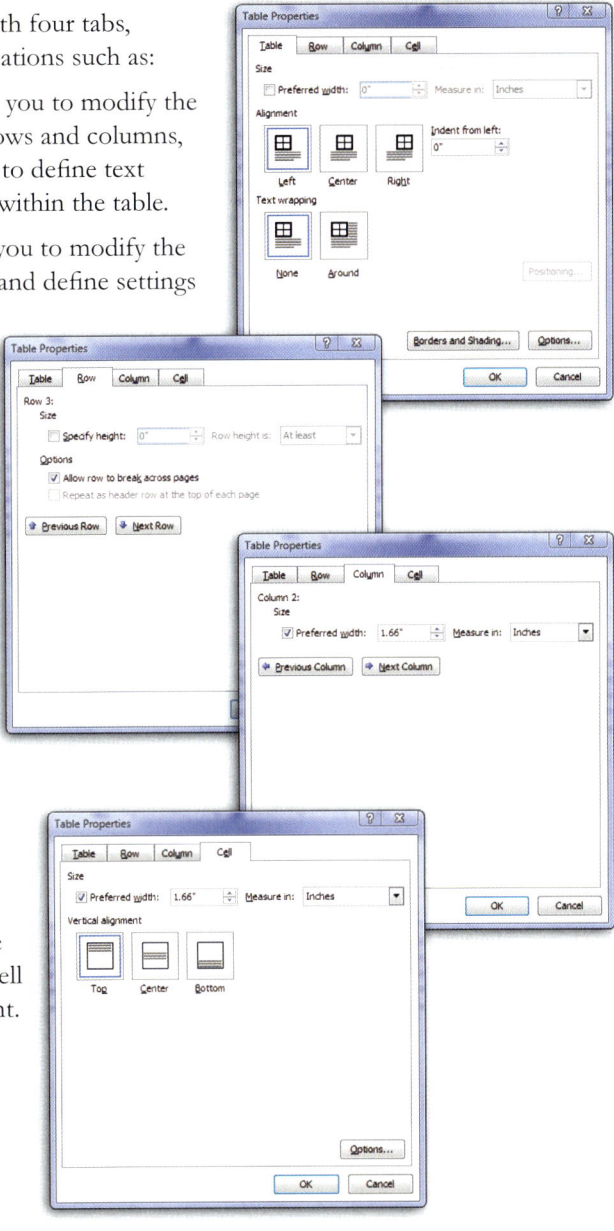

CONTINUE

Format Table Borders, Layout, and Shading   57

17 Format Table Borders, Layout, and Shading (continued)

To Insert Rows or Columns

1. Place cursor in the position where a row or column should be added.

2. Right-click and select **Insert** from the menu.

3. Select option to place a column or row before or after the selected area in the table.

To Merge Cells

1. Highlight the rows or columns to merge together.

2. Right-click and select **Merge Cells**.

3. Note the changes to the way the text is presented.

4. Edit text layout after merging cells to make sure it is formatted correctly.

To Split Cells

1. Highlight a cell you wish to split into multiple columns or rows.

2. Right-click and select **Split Cells**.

3. In the dialog box, select the number of rows and/or columns to split into.

4. Click **OK** to apply.

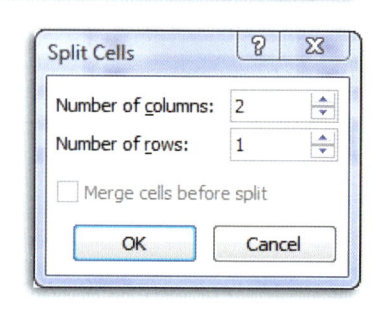

58 QuickClicks: Microsoft Word 2007

design

Format Borders

In tables, "borders" are the lines surrounding cells. The borders in a table always exist—whether they are visible and printed or not. You can modify the visibility, style, color, and width of table borders. To modify borders:

1. Select the cell(s) you want to format.

2. On the **Table Tools Design** tab **A**, click the **Borders** dropdown arrow **B**.

3. Select a border from the menu to either add or remove, or select **Borders and Shading** **C** to customize formatting.

4. In the **Borders and Shading** dialog box, select a border setting, style, color, and width.

5. Specify whether these settings should apply to the **Whole Table** or to the selected cell(s) only in the **Apply to** box.

    *Note: To remove all borders from the cell(s) or Table, click **None** under Setting.*

6. Click **OK** to accept the border settings.

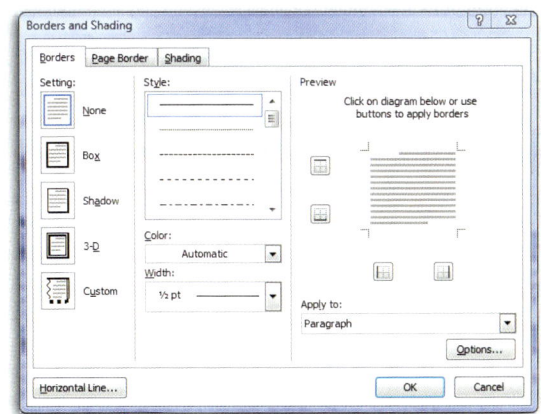

Format Table Borders, Layout, and Shading   59

17 Format Table Borders, Layout, and Shading (continued)

Format Shading

Shading is a design element used to highlight or emphasize certain elements in the presentation of the data. To modify shading:

1. Select the cell(s) you want to format.

2. On the **Table Tools Design** tab, click the **Shading** dropdown arrow **D**.

3. Select a color from the menu for quick shading OR right-click on the selected cells in the table and select **Borders and Shading** from the menu to customize shading.

4. In the **Borders and Shading** dialog box, click the **Shading** tab.

5. Select the fill color and/or patterns to shade the cell(s).

6. Specify whether these settings should apply to the whole table or to the selected cell(s) only in the **Apply to** box.

7. Click **OK** to accept the shading settings.

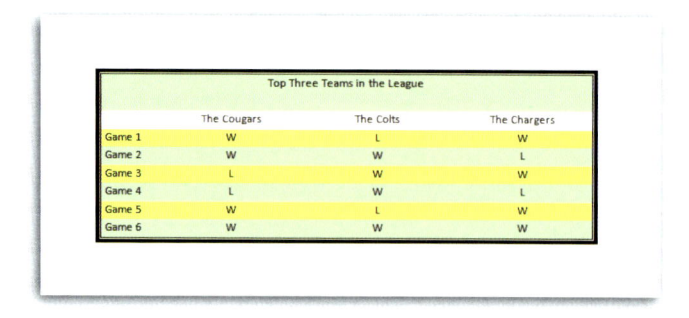

60 QuickClicks: Microsoft Word 2007

design

Format Text

The text within a table can be formatted like any other text in the document. In other words, text elements such as alignment, size, color, and style can be modified.

1. Select the text to be formatted.

2. On the **Home** tab, in the **Font** group, edit the font, size, style, and color of the text by selecting the appropriate font edit tools **E**.

3. On the **Home** tab, in the **Paragraph** group, edit the font alignment and spacing by selecting the appropriate paragraph edit tools **F**.

	Top Three Teams in the League		
	The Cougars	The Colts	The Chargers
Game 1	W	L	W
Game 2	W	W	L
Game 3	L	W	W
Game 4	L	W	L
Game 5	W	L	W
Game 6	W	W	W

Quickest Click: Right-click on the selected cells in the table and select **Borders and Shading** from the menu.

Format Table Borders, Layout, and Shading

18 | Perform Calculations in a Table

Difficulty: ●●○○

PROBLEM You are working with a table of data in your Word project, and you want to insert calculations into the table to add or obtain an average of your numbers.

SOLUTION When using number data in a Word project, there is often a need to perform calculations. While you could perform these math functions on a calculator and simply type them in, this won't maintain accuracy if the figures ever change or if new figures are added.

See Also: Insert and Manage Shared Document Components; Add a Table to a Document; Format Table Borders, Layout, and Shading; Create Templates

> **What Microsoft Calls It:** Insert Formula

Step-by-Step

Calculate a Value in a Table

1. Place the cursor in the cell where the calculation will be performed.

2. Click the **Layout** tab under **Table Tools**.

3. Click the **Formula** button **A** to open the **Formula** dialog box.

   Note: Word will auto-populate a formula based on common calculations that are used.

62   QuickClicks: Microsoft Word 2007

design

4. If the auto-populated format is not the one you need, click the **Paste Function** B dropdown arrow and select a function from the list.

5. To reference the contents of a table cell, type the cell name in the parentheses within the formula. For example, to average the values in cells a1 through a3, the formula would read =Average(a1,a3).

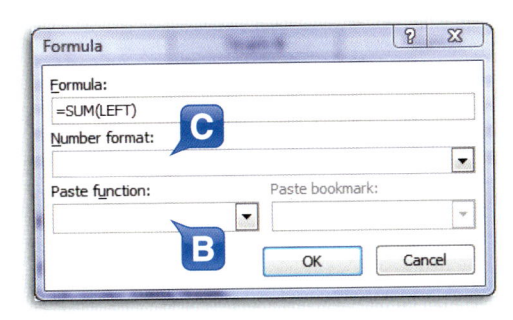

6. In the **Number format** box C, enter a format for the numbers. For example, to display the numbers as a decimal percentage, click 0.00%. Enter 0 to display an average to the nearest whole number. To display a true average, enter 0.00 in the **Number Format** box.

7. Click **OK** to complete.

> **Bright Idea:** If you are doing an operation, such as adding numbers of a column in the last row of the column, you can type =Sum. This will add together the numbers that appear in the column above the cell. If you are doing a similar operation in the last column of a row, you can type =Sum (Left). This will add the numbers that appear in the row to the left of this cell.

> **Hot Tip:** You can insert formulas anywhere in a document, not just in tables. You can also insert fields that update automatically each time you open the document. This can be handy for creating templates.

Perform Calculations in a Table

19 Insert and Manage Stored Document Components

Difficulty: ●●●○

PROBLEM Your organization's senior members are required to submit reports on their segment of the association. It would be helpful if the reporting members had access to standardized document elements (such as headers, footers, and cover pages) to easily access and use.

SOLUTION A **Quick Part** is a defined field or set of fields you can pull into a document. Word calls these building blocks. Building blocks are elements within a document, or element templates that allow you to create standardized documents quickly and easily. These are different from traditional templates because they are document components, as opposed to complete documents. The components are contained in galleries and include such document elements as headers and footers, table of contents, cover pages, text boxes, watermarks, and even boilerplate text.

While Microsoft Word 2007 has default Building Block components available, you can create your own Building Blocks and save them in the Building Blocks gallery (Quick Parts) for use in future documents.

See Also: Perform Calculations in a Table; Create Templates; Insert Text Box

> **What Microsoft Calls It:** Building Blocks/Quick Parts

Step-by-Step

Creating a Building Block Component

1. Select the content you want to save as a building block, such as a custom header.

2. On the **Insert** tab, in the **Text** group, select **Quick Parts** **A**.

3. Click **Save Selection to Quick Part Gallery** **B**.

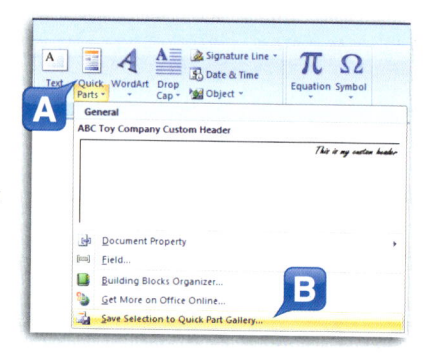

64   QuickClicks: Microsoft Word 2007

design

4. The **Create New Building Block** dialog box appears.

5. Type a name for the Quick Part **C** and click **OK D**.

Adding Custom Building Block Components to Document

1. Open the document that will use the building block component.

2. Place the cursor where the building block component will be added.

3. On the **Insert** tab, in the **Text** group, select **Quick Parts E**.

4. The saved building block component will be listed along with a preview **F**.

5. Select the component and click the **Insert** button to insert at the cursor position.

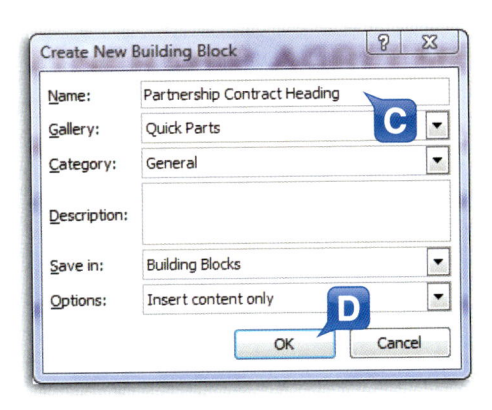

Hot Tip: To view all available building blocks (system default and custom), click the **Building Blocks Organizer** in the **Quick Parts** menu.

Insert and Manage Stored Document Components 65

20 Insert Manual Page Breaks

Difficulty: ●○○○

PROBLEM You are creating a long and complex document that includes pieces written by several different authors. You want each author's work to begin on a new page.

SOLUTION Insert a page break when you want to start a new page. This is useful when you want to separate content in your document. When you insert a page break, the text immediately after your page break will always appear on a new page.

Step-by-Step

1. Select the place in the document where the new page should begin **A**.

2. On the **Insert** tab in the **Pages** group, click **Page Break** **B**.

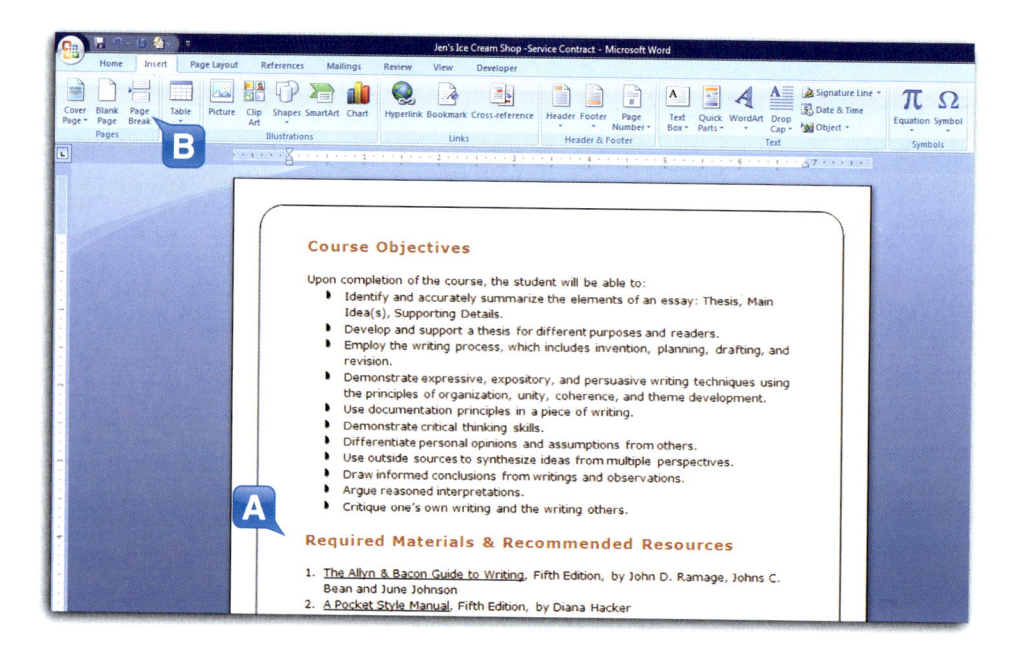

66   QuickClicks: Microsoft Word 2007

design

Original Page

A

After Page Break

Quickest Click: Place your cursor where you want to insert the page break and click **CTRL+Enter**.

Insert Manual Page Breaks

21 Divide Document into Sections

Difficulty: ●●○○

PROBLEM You have created a manual with several chapters, including an introduction. You want to begin page numbering after the introduction.

SOLUTION Section breaks divide your document into separate pieces, or sections. Each section can contain any number of pages and have its own formatting, including different headers and footers. The following elements can be edited separately for each section:

- Margins
- Paper size or orientation
- Paper source for a printer
- Page borders
- Alignment of text on a page
- Headers and footers
- Columns
- Page numbers
- Line numbers
- Foot notes and end notes

See Also: Insert Text or an Image at the Top or Bottom of a Page

> **What Microsoft Calls It:** Section Breaks

Step-by-Step

1. Select the position in the document where the section break will begin.

design

2. On the **Page Layout** tab, in the **Page Setup** group, click **Breaks** **A**.

3. Click the specific type of section break from the following options:

   - **Next Page** **B**: Inserts a section break and starts the new section on the next page. This is useful for starting new chapters in a document.

   - **Continuous** **C**: Inserts a section break and starts the new section on the same page. This is useful when creating a format change, such as utilizing different column layouts on a page.

   - **Even Page** **D**: Inserts a section break and starts the new section on the next even-numbered page. This is useful if you want chapters to always begin on an even page.

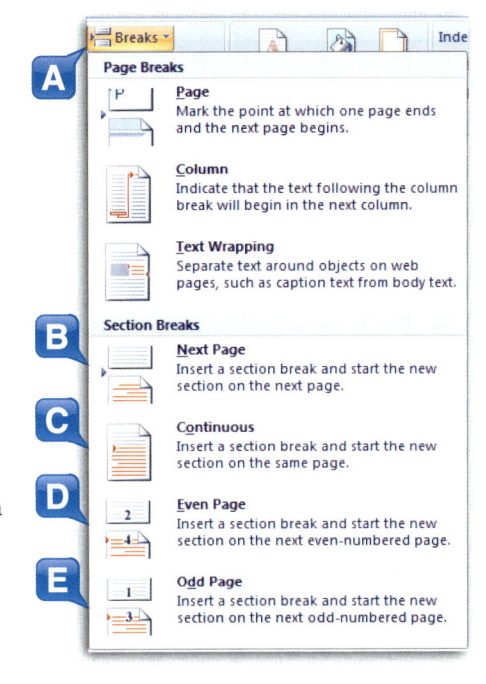

   - **Odd Page** **E**: Inserts a section break and starts the new section on the next odd-numbered page. This is useful if you want chapters to always begin on an odd page, or if facing pages have different footers, such as page numbers in the outside margins.

> **Hot Tip:** Turn on paragraph marks to see where section breaks are located. Click on the **Paragraph Marks** button in the **Paragraph** group on the **Home** tab.

> **Caution:** Section breaks control the formatting of the text that precedes them. When you delete a section break, you also delete the section formatting for the text before the break. That text will become part of the following section and assume all formatting for that section. The break that controls the formatting for the last portion of your document is not displayed as part of the document. To change the document formatting, click in the last paragraph of the document.

Divide Document into Sections   69

22 Insert Text or an Image at the Top or Bottom of a Page

Difficulty: ●●○○

PROBLEM You want to insert your company logo, page numbers, date, file name, or other text at the top and bottom of your document pages.

SOLUTION Text or images that appear in the top or bottom margins of your document are referred to as "headers" and "footers." Headers and footers are sections near the top or bottom margins of each page in a document. They can contain text or graphics. The information contained in these areas can be the same on all pages in a basic document or can differ by section in a more complex document.

Microsoft Word 2007 contains several standard headers and footers that include elements such as page number, file name, document title, author's name, current date, etc. You can also create custom headers and footers. The flexibility of headers and footers is immeasurable, limited only by the requirements of the document and the imagination of the author.

See Also: Divide Document into Sections

> **What Microsoft Calls It:** Insert Header or Footer

Step-by-Step

Use Predefined Header or Footer

1. On the **Insert** tab, in the **Header & Footer** click **Header A** or **Footer B**.

2. Select a header or footer design from the pre-established list **C**.

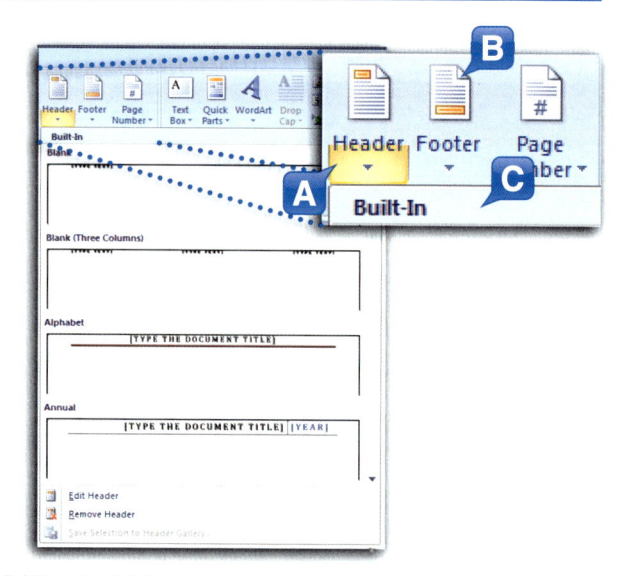

3. The header or footer is inserted on every page of the document.

4. Repeat steps to edit the header and/or footer. Additional elements may be added to the header or footer at any time.

5. To return to the main body of your document, click the **Close Header & Footer** button on the **Header & Footer Tools Design** tab.

Insert Text or an Image at the Top or Bottom of a Page

22 | Insert Text or an Image at the Top or Bottom of a Page (continued)

Create a Custom Header or Footer

1. In the **Header & Footer** group on the **Insert** tab, click **Header** or **Footer**.

2. Click **Edit Header** or **Edit Footer** D.

3. Type text into the header or footer area.

4. To insert an image, use the **Picture** or **Clip Art** buttons under **Header & Footer Tools**, on the **Design** tab, in the **Insert** group E.

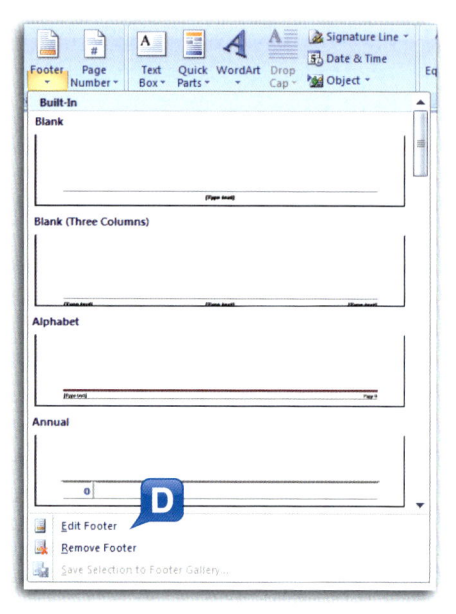

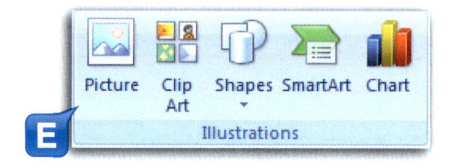

72   QuickClicks: Microsoft Word 2007

design

Quickest Click: Double-click in the very top or bottom area of a page in your document to open the header or footer editing areas. To return to the main body of your document, double-click anywhere in the body section of a page.

Bright Idea 1: There may be instances where the header or footer should not appear on certain pages of the document, such as when the cover page has a different format. Options are included under **Header & Footer** tools, on the **Design** tab.

Bright Idea 2: If the document includes section breaks, each section can contain its own custom header and footer. Options are included under **Header & Footer** tools on the **Design** tab.

Bright Idea 3: You can specify different headers and footers for odd/even pages. This is especially useful when you are printing documents that will open like a book. For example, the header on the left hand page may have a title, and the header on the right hand page may have an author name. Options are included under **Header & Footer Tools**, on the **Design** tab.

Insert Text or an Image at the Top or Bottom of a Page

23 | Insert a Hyperlink in a Document

Difficulty: ●○○○

PROBLEM Your Human Resources department creates and distributes a memo to employees regarding next year's benefit selections. There are several documents that need to be reviewed and some forms to be completed and returned by a certain date. Instead of sending these as attachments via e-mail, which will create a large file size and slow the process, you want to insert links to the additional files, along with instructions and a summary of each in the main document.

SOLUTION Insert hyperlinks to point to other files, web addresses, or locations within the same document. A hyperlink can be assigned to either text or graphics. When you click a hyperlink, the referenced "point to" location opens. These types of links are most often seen on web pages. However, they are frequently used in Word as a way to embed links to other files related to the main source document.

See Also: Mark a Point in a Document for Future Access

Step-by-Step

1. Select the text or the image that will be formatted as a hyperlink.
2. On the **Insert** tab in the **Links** group, click **Hyperlink** **A**.

74   QuickClicks: Microsoft Word 2007

annotate

3. In the **Insert Hyperlink** dialog box, select the **Link to** location **B**:
   - **Existing File or Web Page**: Select this option if you want to link to another Word document on your computer or the network, or if you want to link to a web page.
     » Just to the right of the **Look in** dropdown menu, click the folder icon **C** to browse your computer or the network for a document. Double-click the document you want to link to. The **Insert Hyperlink** box closes and Word creates the link.
     » To link to a Web page, click the Internet icon in the upper-right corner **D** to open your web browser. Go to the web page you want to link to and then go back to the **Insert Hyperlink** box and click the **Existing File** or **Web Page** button. Word adds the address in your web browser to the **Address** box **E**. Click **OK** to close the box and create the hyperlink.

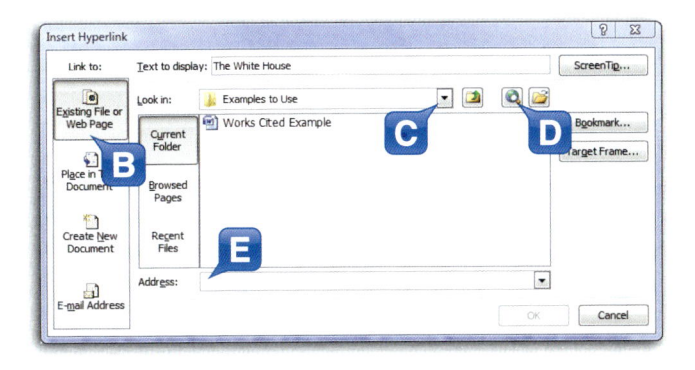

Insert a Hyperlink in a Document   75

23 Insert a Hyperlink in a Document (continued)

- **Place in This Document**: Select this option if you are creating a link to help readers jump around in a long document. Within a document, Word can create links to either headings or bookmarks.

- **Create New Document**: Select this option to create a hyperlink to a document you have not created yet. When you click **Create New Document**, the **Insert Hyperlink** box changes. Type the name of the new document you want to create in the **Name of new document** text box. Click **OK** to save your new document.

- **E-mail Address:** Select this option to create a *mailto* hyperlink in your document. The **Edit Hyperlink** box changes and you can now type the e-mail address that you want hyperlinked **F**.

4. Click the **ScreenTip** button **G** to add a screen tip to the hyperlink. This is text that appears in a box when the user hovers over the hyperlink within a web browser. This is optional.

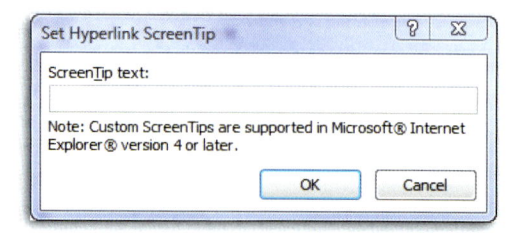

76 QuickClicks: Microsoft Word 2007

annotate

5. In the **Text to Display** box, you can edit the text that is hyperlinked H. For example, if you want to have users click on the words "Click here" instead of the name of the document, you can edit the text in the **Text to Display** box and Word will display this text in the document once you click **OK**.

6. When edits are complete, click **OK** to apply.

7. The text you highlighted is now blue and underlined, indicating that it is an active hyperlink.

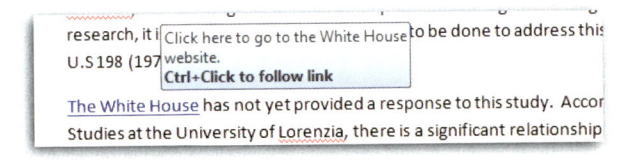

8. Users can **CTRL+click** on the hyperlink to follow the link.

> **Quickest Click:** Select the text to be linked, then right-click and select **Hyperlink** from the menu.

> **Caution:** If you edit the text in the **Text to Display** box, make sure that the text you've entered fits within the context of document. You may have to go back into your document and review/edit to verify.

Insert a Hyperlink in a Document   77

24 Mark a Point in a Document for Future Access

Difficulty: ●○○○

PROBLEM You have created a detailed reference guide. You want to create a way for certain items within the document to be easily and quickly referenced–from a Table of Contents or from other parts of the document.

SOLUTION Use **Bookmarks** or a **Cross Reference** to mark text so that you and your reader can quickly get to it. You can create a named bookmark to indicate a certain place in the document and then reference that bookmark's name in a variety of ways, including cross-referencing or linking. Bookmarks can be created in any section of a document and can reference a specific location, paragraphs of text, or objects. Bookmarks are most typically used for navigation and cross-references.

See Also: Insert a Hyperlink in a Document

What Microsoft Calls It: Bookmarks

Step-by-Step

Create a Bookmark

1. Position the cursor in the place that the bookmark will be inserted **A**.
   - To bookmark a paragraph, position the cursor at the beginning of that paragraph.
   - To bookmark an image or other object, select the image or object.

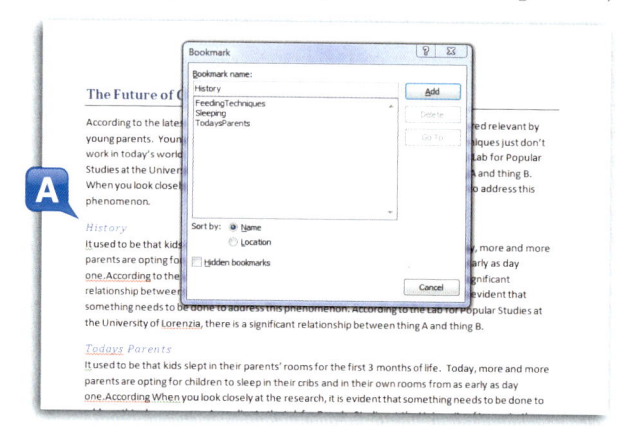

annotate

2. On the **Insert** tab, in the **Links** group, select **Bookmark** B.

3. In the **Bookmark** dialog box, type a name for the bookmark C.
   - Bookmark names can be up to 40 characters and *can* include letters and/or numbers.
   - Spaces and symbols *cannot* be used.

4. Click **Add** to create the bookmark D.

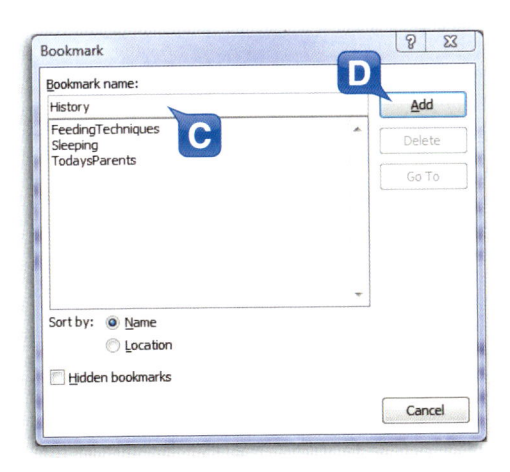

Mark a Point in a Document for Future Access   79

24 Mark a Point in a Document for Future Access (continued)

Browse by Bookmark

On the **Home** tab, in the **Editing** group, click **Go To** to see the bookmarks you created. Use these bookmarks to jump through your document.

Hyperlinks

When you create a hyperlink to a specific point in your document, Word needs something to anchor the link to. That can be a heading or a bookmark that you have already created.

Cross-Reference

Documents can use cross-references to refer to photos, charts, tables, or other parts of the document. They direct the reader to related information located elsewhere in the document.

1. Select the text that starts the cross-reference in the document.

2. On the **References** tab, click the **Cross-Reference** button **E**.

annotate

3. Click the **References type** dropdown arrow **F** and select the type of reference you're linking to (bookmark, footnote, heading, etc.).

4. Click the **Insert reference to** dropdown arrow **G** and select the type of data (page, paragraph number, etc.) that you want to reference.

5. Click the specific item, by number, that you want referenced.

6. To let users click to this item, select the **Insert as hyperlink** check box **H**.

7. To include data regarding the relative position of the referenced item, select the Include above/below check box.

8. Click **Insert** **I**.

9. Repeat steps for additional cross-references.

10. Click **Close** to finish.

Mark a Point in a Document for Future Access   81

25 Create a Table of Contents

Difficulty: ●●○○

PROBLEM You have created a detailed proposal for a client. Since the document is split into separate sections, you want the client to easily find the information he needs without having to scroll through the document page by page.

SOLUTION A Table of Contents allows you to quickly find a section and page number, then go immediately to it without having to scroll or page through the document. You can easily create a Table of Contents by applying preset Heading Styles to your text. Microsoft Word 2007 searches for headings that match the style that you have applied, and inserts the heading text into the Table of Contents.

See Also: Apply Styles to Text

> **What Microsoft Calls It:** Bookmarks

Step-by-Step

Word 2007, by default, uses Heading 1 as the first-level entry in the Table of Contents. Subheadings, using Heading 2 and so forth, would appear in subsequent order.

1. Select the text (formatted as a heading or title/subtitle) that you want to appear in the Table of Contents **A**.

2. On the **Home** tab, in the **Styles** group, select a style for the heading **B**.

82 QuickClicks: Microsoft Word 2007

annotate

3. Repeat these steps (select heading and a heading style) for all the titles/subtitles you want to appear in the Table of Contents.

4. Place the cursor in the area you want the Table of Contents to appear. This is typically the beginning of the document or in between a cover page and the start of the text.

5. On the **References** tab, in the **Table of Contents** group, click **Table of Contents** C.

6. Select a style for the Table of Contents D.

7. As you edit your document and add or delete text and headings, the page numbers and items for the Table of Contents may change. To update the Table of Contents, select the **Table of Contents** object in your document and click the **Update Table** button located at the top of the object.

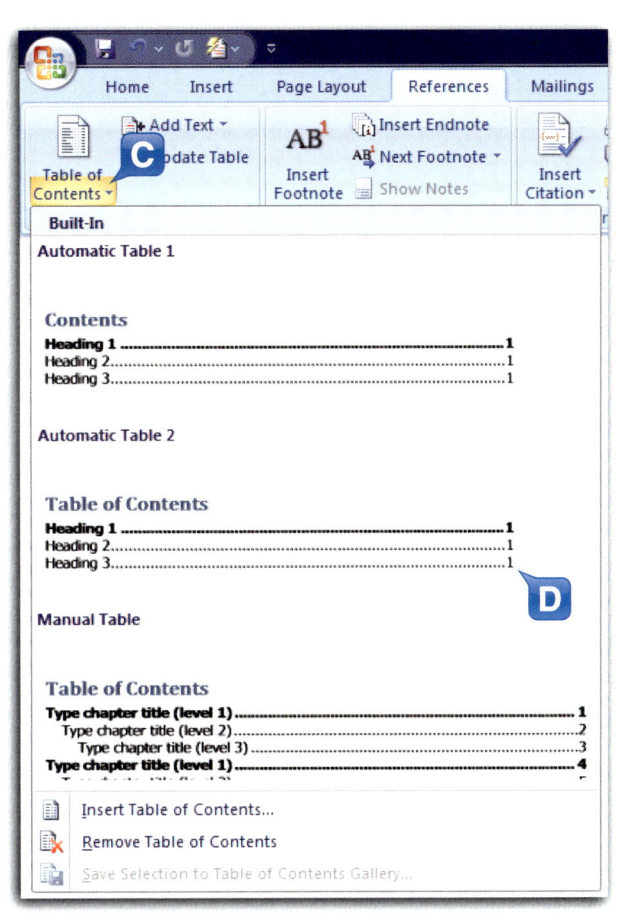

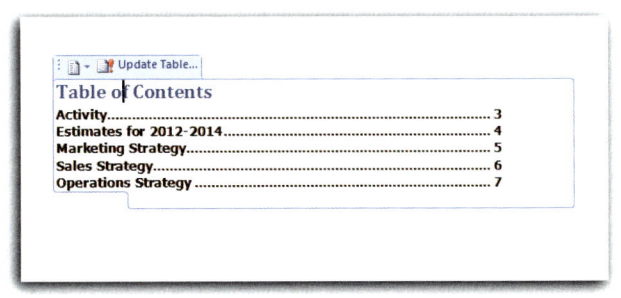

Create a Table of Contents   83

25 Create a Table of Contents (continued)

8. Select the option to update the entire table or just the page numbers. If heading text has been added or deleted, choose to update the entire table so those edits will be accounted for in the Table of Contents.

9. To remove a Table of Contents from your document, click the **Table of Contents** button on the **References** tab in the **Table of Contents** group and click **Remove Table of Contents** E.

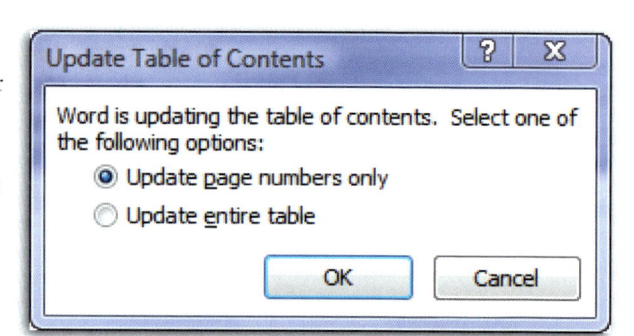

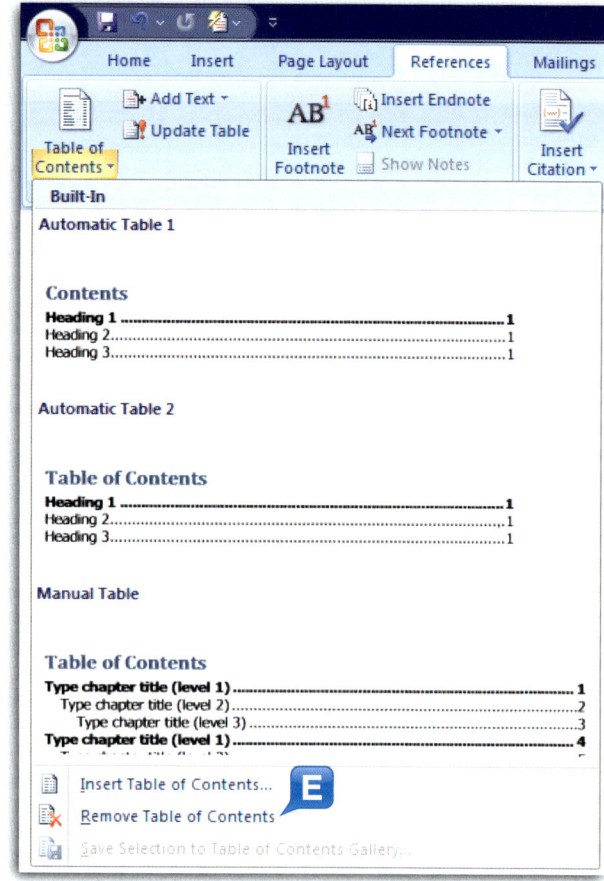

84   QuickClicks: Microsoft Word 2007

annotate

Hot Tip: Hyperlink your Table of Contents headings to the sections they reference. This allows you to easily and quickly access those sections of your document. See the **Insert a Hyperlink** tip for more details.

Quickest Click: To change the style of the Table of Contents in your document, click the **Table of Contents** button on the **References** tab in the **Table of Contents** group and select a different style option. This will simply replace the current Table of Contents style with the new style.

Bright Idea: If you want to include text in the Table of Contents that is not formatted as a heading, select the text and click **Add Text** in the **Table of Contents** group on the **References** tab.

26 Create an Index

Difficulty: ●●○○

PROBLEM You have been asked to create a technical user guide for customers. The customers have indicated that they will not read the user guide from front to back, but instead will look for the items they need and go directly to the pages they are interested in.

SOLUTION An index lists words and topics that appear in a document, as well as their page numbers. An index can be created for individual words, for topics that span multiple pages, or for items that refer to other terms in the document. An index is useful when publishing a large document, such as a detailed report, a technical user guide, or a book manuscript. The index helps readers find a specific topic or term easily and quickly. Creating an index is a three-part process: first, items for entry are marked; second, a design for your index is selected; and last, the index is built.

See Also: Mark a Point in a Document for Future Access

Step-by-Step

Mark and Format Entries for Index

1. In the document, highlight a word or phrase to be indexed.

2. On the **References** tab, in the **Index** group, click **Mark Entry**.

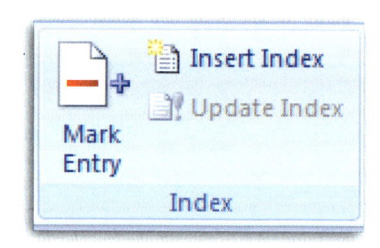

86 QuickClicks: Microsoft Word 2007

annotate

3. In the **Mark Entry** dialog box, verify the content in the **Main Entry** field **A**.

    Note: The text does not have to appear exactly the same way it appears in the document. You can highlight an abbreviation, for example, but display the full term in the index.

4. Create a **Subentry** **B**, or **Cross-reference**, to another entry. These are optional fields.

    - **Cross-reference**: Refers to another index entry. For example, select the word "house" and then type "home" in the cross-reference box. The index entry looks like this: "house, See home."

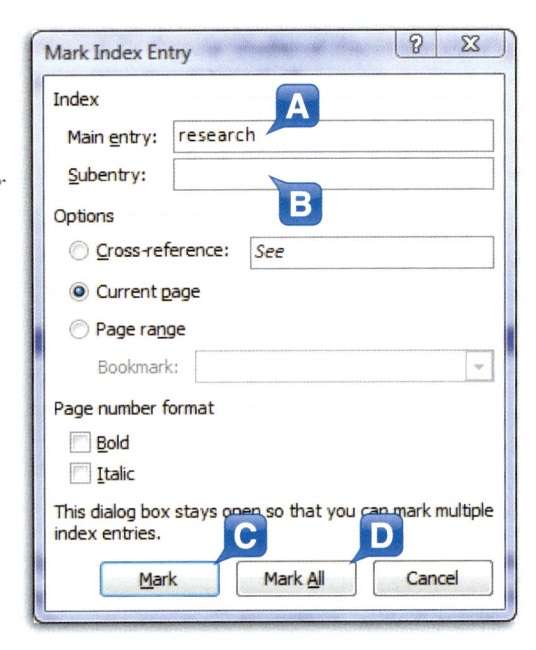

    - **Current page**: Use to index individual words, phrases, or symbols.

    - **Page range**: Use for entries that span more than one page. Select **Page range**, and then select a bookmark from the **Bookmark** dropdown menu.

    Note: Before you can mark a Page range index, you must create a bookmark. Select the text and click ALT+N+K.

5. Format the page numbers that will appear in the index by clicking the **Bold** or **Italic** check box under **Page number format**.

6. Mark the index entry by clicking the **Mark** button **C**. To mark all appearances of the text in the entire document, click the **Mark All** button **D**.

7. To mark additional index entries, follow steps 1-6 until complete.

Create an Index   87

Create an Index (continued)

Build Index

1. Place cursor where the index will appear. Typically, this is at the end of a document.

2. On the **References** tab, in the **Index** group, click **Insert Index**.

3. Select a design in the **Formats** dropdown box **E**. A preview will appear in the preview pane above.

4. Once selected, click **OK** **F**.

Update Index

If you marked additional text and made changes to your document after your index was created, follow these steps to update the index:

1. Place your cursor anywhere within the index **G**.

2. Click **Update Index** in the **Index** group on the **References** tab **H**.

3. Microsoft Word will re-read all the index entries to include any changes.

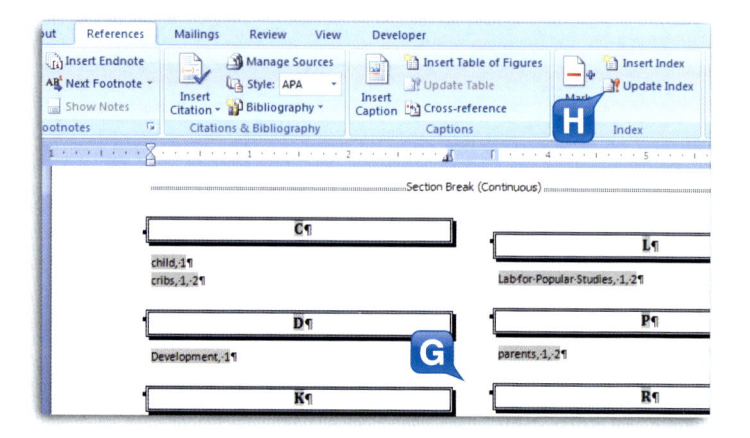

88 QuickClicks: Microsoft Word 2007

annotate

Quickest Click: To open the **Mark Index Entry** dialog box, press **Alt+Shift+X**.

Quickest Click: To update the index, press the **F9 Key** or **ALT+S+D**.

Hot Tip: To format the index text, select the text in the **Main entry** or **Subentry** box. Right-click and select **Font**. Select the formatting.

Caution: Look out for words that appear often, but lack relevance.

Bright Idea: To select a range of text that spans for several pages, click **Bookmark** on the **Insert** tab, in the **Links** group. In the **Bookmark name** box, type a name. Click **Add**. Mark the entry using steps above.

Create an Index

27 Create a Document Summary

Difficulty: ●●●○

PROBLEM You have created a long report and want to include a summary that will highlight the key points of the document and make it easy for a reviewer to get the main idea before reading through all the detail.

SOLUTION Microsoft Word 2007 includes a feature called **AutoSummarize**, which calls out key points in the document. This function works by scanning the document and providing a "score" to each sentence. Sentences that contain words used frequently in the document are given a higher score. The highest-scoring sentences are then displayed in the summary.

This feature allows you to choose whether to highlight key points in a document, insert an executive summary or an abstract, or show only the summary data in the document. AutoSummarize is useful for highly structured documents, such as reports, manuals, and scientific analyses.

See Also: Divide a Document into Sections; Apply a Consistent Look and Feel to a Document; Customize the Quick Access Toolbar and Status Bar

Step-by-Step

The **AutoSummary Tools** must be added to the **Quick Access Toolbar**.

1. Click the **Microsoft Office Button**.
2. Click **Word Options**.
3. Click **Customize**.
4. Select **Choose commands from** and click **All Commands**.
5. Select **AutoSummary Tools** from list of commands.
6. Click **Add**.
7. Click **OK**.

annotate

Insert Summary

1. In the document you want to summarize, click the **AutoSummary Tools** button in the **Quick Access Toolbar**.

2. Click **AutoSummarize**.

3. Select the type of summary to use:
   - Highlight key points.
   - Create a new document and put the summary there.
   - Insert an executive summary or abstract at the top of the document.
   - Hide everything but the summary without leaving the original document.

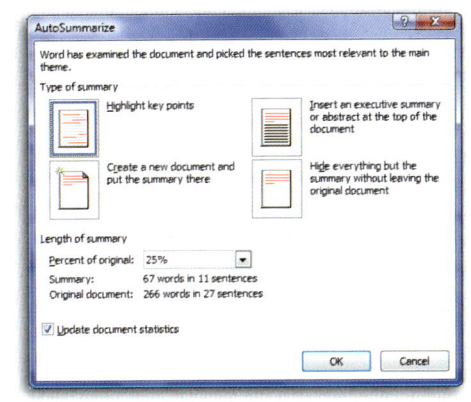

4. In the **Percent of original** box, select the level of detail to include or type in an amount. The higher the percentage, the more detail included.

5. Click **OK** to create the summary.

6. After the summary is created, edit it as needed to polish and refine for publishing.

> **Caution:** AutoSummarize will replace your existing keywords and comments in document properties unless you uncheck the **Update document statistics** check box. The AutoSummary should be carefully proofread for accuracy and clarity before publishing.

> **Bright Idea:** You can easily add a cover page to your document with a built-in Word feature. Click the **Cover Page** dropdown button in the **Pages** group on the **Insert** tab and then select the layout you like. If you have applied a document **Theme**, the theme colors and fonts will automatically be added to your selected cover.

Create a Document Summary

28 Insert a Footnote or Endnote

Difficulty: ●○○○

PROBLEM You have created a long document that references several sources of information. You want to reference these sources, but do not want to create a long, formal bibliography at the end of your document. Instead, you want to display these less rigorous references at the bottom of each page or at the end of the document.

SOLUTION Footnotes and endnotes are ways to cite sources in a document. The difference between a footnote and an endnote is location. Footnotes are displayed at the bottom of the page that the reference appears. Endnotes are displayed at the end of the document or section.

Step-by-Step

Insert a Footnote

1. Place your cursor after the text you want your footnote to reference.

2. On the **References** tab, in the **Footnotes** group, click the **Insert Footnote** [A] button. Word inserts a reference mark at the insertion point and then jumps to the bottom of the page and places a footnote reference.

3. Type the footnote text.

92 QuickClicks: Microsoft Word 2007

annotate

Insert an Endnote

1. Place your cursor after the text you want your endnote to reference.

2. On the **References** tab, in the **Footnotes** group, select **Insert Endnote** **B**.

3. Word inserts a reference mark at the insertion point and then jumps to the end of the document and places a new endnote reference.

4. Type the endnote text.

Format a Footnote or Endnote

1. Place your cursor in the section where you want to change the footnote or endnote format.

2. On the **References** tab, in the **Footnotes** group, click the **Footnote & Endnote** dialog box launcher **C**.

3. Click the **Number format** menu and then select the format you want **D**.

4. To change the starting point, click the **Start at** up or down arrows **E**.

5. Click **Apply change to** and select **Whole document** **F**.

6. Click **Apply** **G** and then click **Cancel** **H** to close.

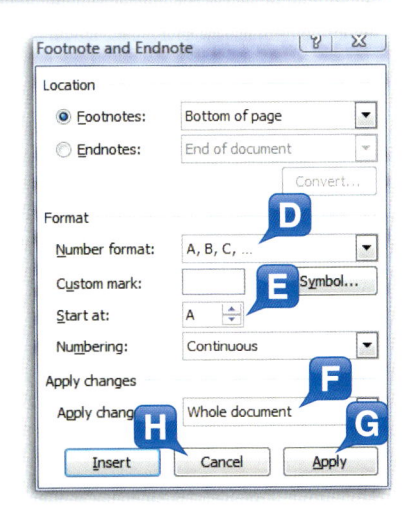

Insert a Footnote or Endnote   93

29 Correctly Cite Sources in a Document

Difficulty: ●●○○

PROBLEM You are writing a long paper or report that references a variety of books, articles, and other resources. You need to create a works cited page to correctly cite the sources used in your document.

SOLUTION Create a bibliography. A bibliography typically appears at the end of a document and provides information about the sources of your cited references. When you create a bibliography, you can choose a standard style, such as APA or MLA, which is widely used in organizations and universities. To create a bibliography, you will first enter the source data (such as the title, author, and date of publication) and then cite them in the document with just a few clicks.

> **What Microsoft Calls It:** Insert Citation; Manage Sources

Step-by-Step

Entering Sources

1. Select a citation style from the dropdown list on the **References** tab, in the **Citations & Bibliography** group **A**.

2. Click the **Manage Sources** button **B**.

3. In the **Source Manager** dialog box, click **New C**.

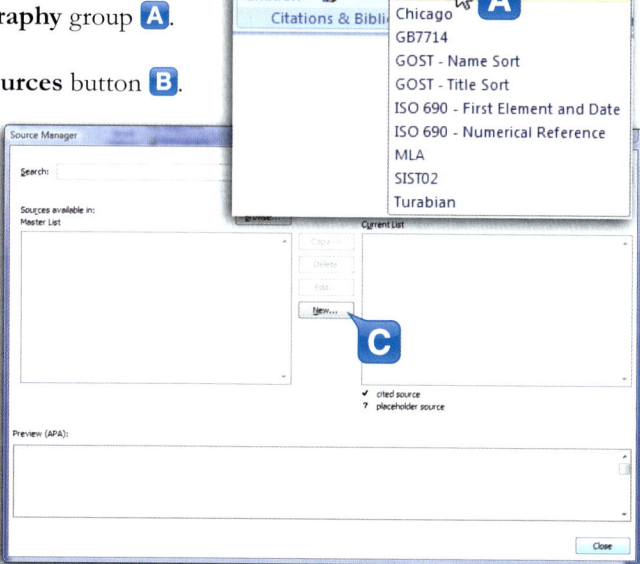

94   QuickClicks: Microsoft Word 2007

annotate

4. In the **Create Source** dialog box, open the **Type of Source** dropdown list and select type (i.e. Book, Journal Article, etc.) **D**.

5. Enter the Author's name **E** in one of two formats:
   - First Middle Last
   - Last, First Middle
   - If there is more than one author, separate names with semicolons.

6. If the author is an organization, mark the **Corporate Author** check box and enter the organization's name.

7. Click the **Edit** button **F** to enter each part of the name in the boxes provided.
   - If there is only one author, click **OK**.
   - If there are multiple authors, click **Add** **G** after each and click **OK** **H** when complete.

8. Complete additional fields for the selected source type.

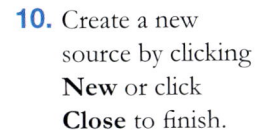

9. Click **OK** to return to the **Source Manager** dialog box **I**.

10. Create a new source by clicking **New** or click **Close** to finish.

Correctly Cite Sources in a Document   95

29 Correctly Cite Sources in a Document (continued)

Insert In-Line References

An in-line reference to a source is inserted using parentheses. The style of these references differs based upon the citation style you are using as well as the source type. These generally include at least the name of the Author, and often the Year, Title, or Page Number.

1. Place cursor in the position where your citation should appear.

2. On the **References** tab, in the **Citations & Bibliography** group, click **Insert Citation**.

3. A menu lists all the sources in the current document.

4. Click the source that applies.

5. A reference to the source will be added as a field J.

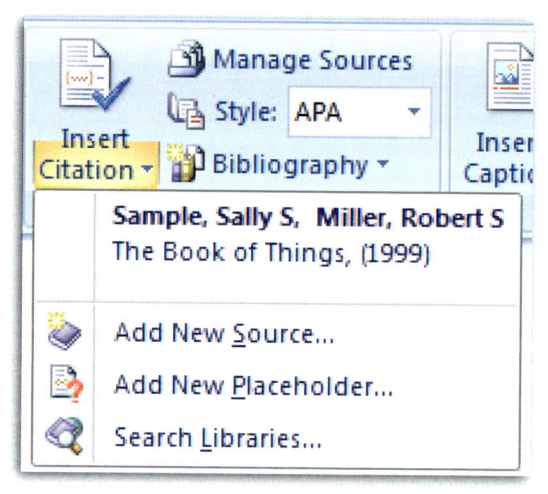

annotate

Generate Bibliography

1. Place the cursor where the bibliography should appear (typically at the end of your document).

2. On the **References** tab, in the **Citations & Bibliography** group, click **Bibliography** K.

3. Click the gallery entry that best represents the bibliography you want to create.

Bright Idea: If you're writing a document and need to cite a source, but don't have the details at hand, you can create a temporary placeholder for the source and then complete the details later in the Source Manager. This allows for maximum productivity. Just remember to name your placeholder something that you can easily identify later.

30 Create a Table of Authorities

Difficulty: ●●○○

PROBLEM You have created a lengthy legal document for a partnering law firm to review prior to an upcoming case. You need to create a table of authorities to reference past cases and rulings in the document for faster and more efficient review.

SOLUTION A Table of Authorities is a list of references (such as cases, statutes, and rulings) in a legal document and the page numbers where the references appear. Start by marking the citations. Citations are different from footnotes and bibliography entries because they are almost exclusively used by the legal industry. Word simplifies the process of adding citations in-line with the text and then bundles them into a master reference called the Table of Authorities.

Step-by-Step

Mark Citations

1. Select the first citation in the document **A**.

    - For example, select "Smith v Jones, 257 U.S 198 (1972)"

2. On the **References** tab, in the **Table of Authorities** group, click **Mark Citation B**.

98   QuickClicks: Microsoft Word 2007

annotate

3. In the **Mark Citation** dialog box, edit the text if necessary **C**.

4. Open the **Category** dropdown menu **D** and select the type of citation (cases, statutes, etc.)

5. In the **Short Citation** box, enter a short version of the citation. The default is a copy of the selected text **E**.

6. Click **Mark** **F**.

7. The selected text now appears in the **Long Citation** box **G**. 🔥

8. To mark another citation, click **Next Citation**.

9. Repeat steps until all citations have been marked.

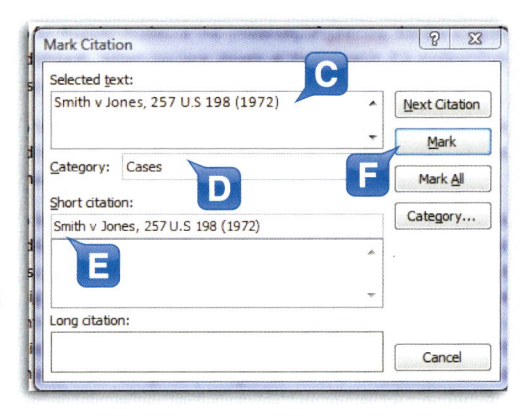

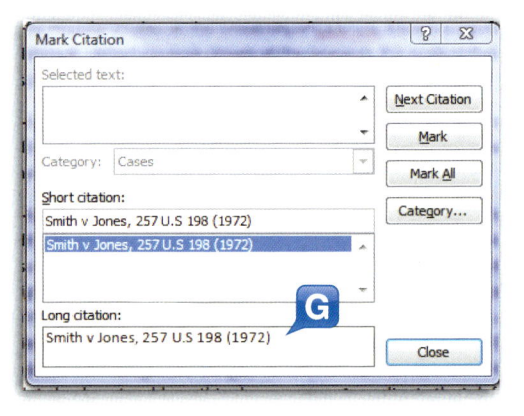

CONTINUE

Create a Table of Authorities 99

30 Create a Table of Authorities (continued)

Create Table of Authorities

1. Position the cursor where the table should appear.

2. On the **References** tab, in the **Table of Authorities** group, click **Insert Table of Authorities** H.

3. In the **Table of Authorities** dialog box, setting options are as follows:
   - **Use Passim**: When listing citations that appear frequently in the same document, it is standard to substitute the word *passim* for the multiple references. Word, by default, uses *passim* after at least five references to the same citation appear. Uncheck the checkbox if you want to display the actual page numbers in each instance instead.
   - **Keep Original Formatting**: Some citations contain character formatting that carries, by default, into the Table of Authorities. If you do not want the formatting to carry over, uncheck the checkbox.
   - **Tab leader**: Select the leader type or "none."
   - **Formats**: Select one of the style sets or use **From Template** to match the style set that the document uses.
   - **Category**: This defaults to **ALL** J. Narrow this down by selecting.

annotate

- Click **Modify** to modify the styles used for the **Table of Authorities**. This is optional.
- Click **OK** to apply modifications and create the table of authorities.

Cases

Smith v Jones, 257 U.S 198 (1972) 1

Hot Tip: If you want Word to scan the entire document and mark all references to the same citation, short and long, click **Mark All**.

Caution: If you add more citations to a legal document after your table of authorities has been created, you may want to delete the existing table and create a new one to ensure that the new citations are displayed properly.

Create a Table of Authorities

31 | Customize the Quick Access Toolbar and Status Bar

Difficulty: ●●○○

PROBLEM There are several actions and commands you use frequently, but they are spread across multiple tabs and often several clicks deep. It would be helpful if they were available in one convenient menu.

SOLUTION The **Quick Access** toolbar is a row of buttons in the top-left corner of the Word window. This toolbar can be repositioned either above or below the Ribbon and can be customized. Buttons can be added, removed, or rearranged. The **Status Bar** is the bar at the bottom of the Word window. The status bar contains items such as page status, word count, page view buttons, and a zoom slide button.

Customizing the **Quick Access toolbar** or the **Status bar** allows you to quickly perform tasks that are not necessarily available through a shortcut key or available by clicking the Ribbon. Since utilizing this customization option is a highly individualized task, the variations are limitless.

See Also: Record and Play Back a Series of Actions

Step-by-Step

Customize the Quick Access Toolbar

1. Click the **Microsoft Office** button.

2. Select **Word Options**.

3. Click **Customize** **A**.

4. Open the **Choose Commands From** list **B** and make a selection from the **Choose Commands From** dropdown:

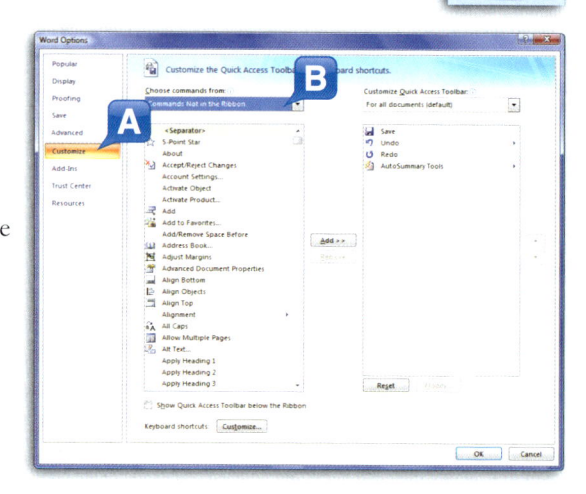

102 QuickClicks: Microsoft Word 2007

accelerate

- **Popular commands**: This includes commands that Word users most frequently use in the **Quick Access Toolbar**, such as **Save**, **Open**, **New**, and **Print Preview**.
- **Commands not in the ribbon**: This includes features that either were available in a previous version of Word or only pertain to specific types of projects and are less frequently used. Microsoft did not put these commands on the 2007 ribbon.
- **All commands**: This includes a list of all available commands.
- **Macros**: This includes a list of all available macros.

5. Select a command **C**.

6. Click **Add** **D**.

7. Add more commands as desired.

8. Click **OK** **E**.

Customize the Status Bar

1. Right-click the **Status Bar** **F**.

2. A menu opens with check marks next to the displayed items **G**.

3. Click an item to toggle it on or off.

4. Checked items are active and visible on the toolbar.

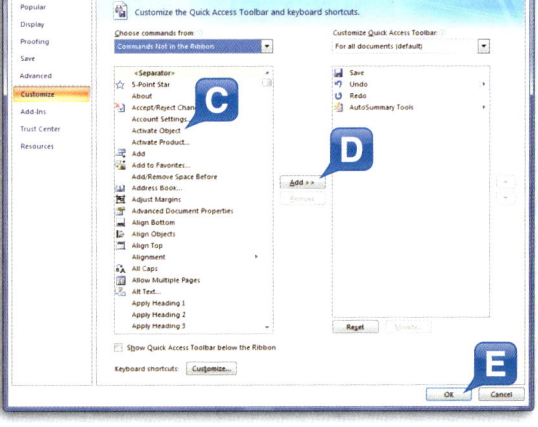

Customize the Quick Access Toolbar and Status Bar   103

32 Create Templates

Difficulty: ●●●○

PROBLEM You send daily updates that need to include your organization's branding, colors, fonts, logo, and corporate tagline. Currently, you save an old formatted document, and do a "Save As" to edit all the text within the document. This is proving to be ineffective, as you have made mistakes by not deleting all the old text appropriately. You want to create a template to make the creation of these documents simple and clean.

SOLUTION Templates are documents that are predesigned and preformatted to serve as the foundations for other documents. Each template is made up of styles that have common design elements, such as fonts, sizes, colors, and layout. Templates can also contain styles and even preset text, if desired.

See Also: Appendix: Save a Document to the Appropriate File Format; Create a Form with Fillable Fields; Perform Calculations in a Table; Insert and Manage Stored Document Components

Step-by-Step

Create a Template

Enter all your necessary information into a new document, such as formatting and graphics. You can enter generic text as a placeholder. However, this is a matter of preference. Some people prefer to work with a clean slate to prevent errors. This decision should be driven by the content you are working with and your preferences.

1. Click the **Microsoft Office** button.
2. Click **Save As**.

accelerate

3. In the **Save As** dialog box, select template type:

   - **Word Template**: Select this to create a template for Word 2007.

   - **Word Macro-Enabled Template**: Select this to create a template for Word 2007 with macros.

   - **Word 97-2003 Template**: Select this to create a template for Word versions 97 through 2003.

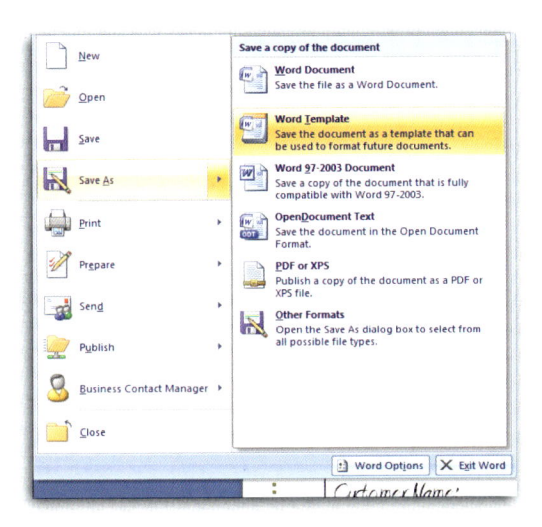

4. Microsoft Office templates are typically stored in the following location:

   - **Windows Vista and 7**: C:\Users\Your Name\AppData\Roaming\Microsoft\Templates

   - **WindowsXP**: C:\Documents and Settings\Your Name\Application Data\Microsoft\Templates

   Note: You can save your template to any location on your computer, or on your network if the template will be used by others in your organization.

5. Click **Save**.

Create Templates 105

Create Templates (continued)

Use a Template to Create New Document

1. Click the **Microsoft Office** button.

2. Click **Open** and click the **Files of typ**e dropdown arrow.

3. Select **Templates**.

4. Click the **Look in** dropdown arrow and select the drive and folder that contains the template you want to open.

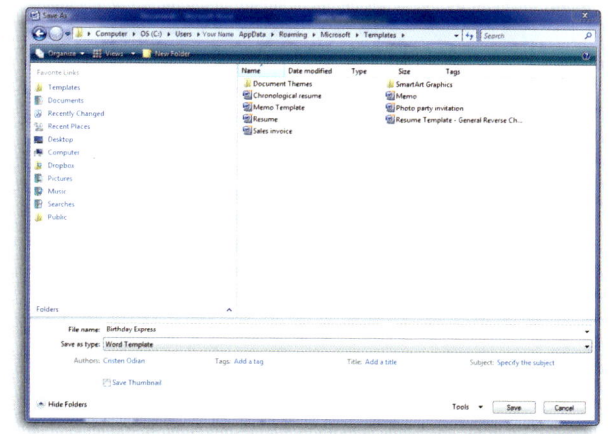

Note: Use this guide to locate where Microsoft Office typically stores templates. If you stored it in another location, browse to locate and select the template.

5. Click the file name of your template.

6. Click **Open**.

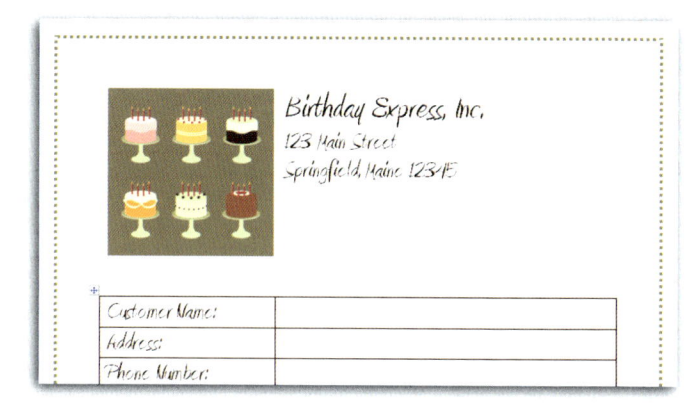

106 QuickClicks: Microsoft Word 2007

accelerate

Hot Tip: Whether you are using a custom template or not, every document is based upon a template. When you open a template, the template itself does not change as you enter data into the new document. Word starts a new document that contains the formatting, graphics, and text contained in the template. To save your new document, choose **Save As**.

33 Locate and Substitute Words, Formatting, Terms, and Objects in a Document

Difficulty: ●●○○

PROBLEM You realize that you have text in your document that you need to change. You have spelled the name "Ann" (one of your customers) incorrectly throughout your 50 page document. You need to replace her name with the correct spelling, "Anne." You do not want to do it manually, because you might miss an occurrence within the document.

SOLUTION There are a variety of ways to locate content in a document. The **Find** feature helps locate instances of a specified string of text. It can also locate specific formatting, or a non-printing symbol or code. You can search for tabs or paragraph breaks as well as phone numbers or names beginning with certain letters. The **Replace** feature then takes the next step of replacing the found item with a different text string. There are a variety of useful functions in the **Editing** tool.

> **What Microsoft Calls It:** Find and Replace

Step-by-Step

Basic Find and Replace

1. On the **Home** tab in the **Editing** group, click **Find**.
2. Type the text string into the **Find What** box **A**.
3. Click **Find Next** **B**.
4. The display jumps to the first instance of the text in your document.
5. To replace text, click the **Replace** tab **C**.

108 QuickClicks: Microsoft Word 2007

accelerate

6. Enter text to replace original in the **Replace with** box **D**.

7. Click **Replace** **E**.

8. Click **Find Next** until Word has finished searching the document **F**. ⚠

Find and Replace Formatting in the Document

The **Find and Replace Formatting in the Document** feature allows you to find text or other elements with specific font, paragraph, tab, language, frame, style, or highlight attributes. The **Reading Highlight** button highlights items found to make them easier to read.

1. In the **Find and Replace** dialog box, click the **More** button **G** to display additional **Find** options **H**.

2. Click the **Format** button **I** to open the formatting menu.

3. Select the type of formatting to specify. For example, to specify character formatting such as a font, click Font.

4. In the corresponding dialog box, specify the type of formatting you want to find.

5. Click **OK**.

    Note: The dialog box and options will differ based on the formatting menu item you choose.

6. In the **Find and Replace** dialog box, descriptive text appears under the **Find what** box identifying the formatting chosen for the **Find** action **J**.

7. Continue the find and/or replace operations as normal.

CONTINUE

Locate and Substitute Words, Formatting, Terms, and Objects in a Document   **109**

33 | Locate and Substitute Words and Terms in a Document (continued)

Find and Replace Special Characters

The **Find and Replace Special Characters** feature is useful, for example, if you want to replace all single paragraph breaks in a document with double paragraph breaks.

1. In the **Find and Replace** dialog box, click the **More** button [More >>] to display additional **Find** options.

2. Click the **Special** button.

3. Select a function to use in the **Find** action.

4. Continue the **Find** and/or **Replace** operations as normal.

Use Select Browse Object

The **Select Browse Object** feature provides a quick way to scroll through a document when you are looking for specific content. This will skip over areas of the document that do not contain the object(s) you are trying to find.

1. On the **Home** tab, in the **Editing** group, click **Select**.

2. Choose **Select Objects**, **Select All**, or **Select Text with Similar Formatting**.

Use Go To

The **Go To** feature is useful when you want to jump to a specific instance of a content type–but not browse all instances. **Go To** allows you to enter the page number you want to jump to and go directly to the item on that page. This also works with objects such as comments, bookmarks, and graphics. For example, if you want to quickly review all comments that have been added to a document, use the **Go To** feature to save time in editing.

1. On the **Home** tab, in the **Editing** group, click **Find**.

2. Select **Go To**.

accelerate

3. Select the element **J** to use in the search and specify the detail requested.

4. Click **Next K** to jump to your requested data.

> **Caution: Replace All** is a quick way to substitute text throughout the entire document. However, you must be careful that the string of text does not exist as a part of any other words in the document. For example, you are using the **Find and Replace** function to replace the misspelled name *Ann* with *Anne*. If you have the word *Annuity* in your document, the **Replace All** function will change your word to *Anneuity*. To correct for this, make sure you choose to replace "Ann " (with a space after the second "n") with "Anne " (with a space after the "e"). This will allow you to make the replacement without introducing additional errors.

> **Hot Tip:** If you think you have overused a word and you want to quickly search the document to find all instances of the word, select the word in the document. Click the **Find** button in the **Editing** group on the **Home** tab. Click **Reading Highlight** and **Highlight All**. You can clear the highlights by selecting **Clear Highlighting**.

> **Quickest Click:** Click the **Select Browse Object** button or **ALT+CTRL+HOME** to bring up the **Select Browse** command menu. The icons represent the following actions to browse:
> - Go To
> - Find
> - By Edits
> - By Heading
> - By Graphic
> - By Table
> - By Field
> - By Endnote
> - By Footnote
> - By Comment
> - By Section
> - By Page

Locate and Substitute Words, Formatting, Terms, and Objects in a Document   111

34 | Use AutoCorrect to Save Time and Prevent Errors

Difficulty: ●●○○

PROBLEM You often mistype the name of your organization's research facility, Joulette Thomatican Laboratory.

SOLUTION AutoCorrect is a function that automatically replaces all instances of a certain text string with another. By setting **AutoCorrect** options, you can save time by automatically correcting typos within a document. In this example, set the AutoCorrect option so you can type *JT Lab* and Word will autocorrect it to display *Joulette Thomatican Laboratory*. Because the corrections are made automatically, you will not need to edit these later.

Step-by-Step

Setting AutoCorrect Options

1. Click the **Microsoft Office** button.

2. Select **Word Options**.

3. Click **Proofing** A.

4. Click **AutoCorrect Options** button B.

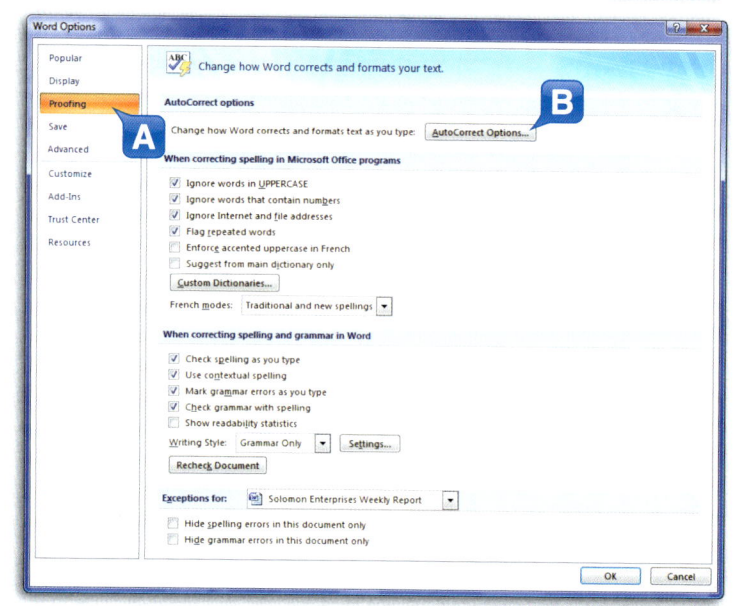

112   QuickClicks: Microsoft Word 2007

accelerate

5. The top portion of the **AutoCorrect** tab contains check boxes for enabling/disabling certain features.

- **Show AutoCorrect Options Buttons**: Clear this to prevent the AutoCorrect Options button from appearing after an AutoCorrect action.

- **Correct TWo INitial CApitals**: If a word starts out with two capital letters and then switches to lowercase, AutoCorrect will lowercase the second letter.

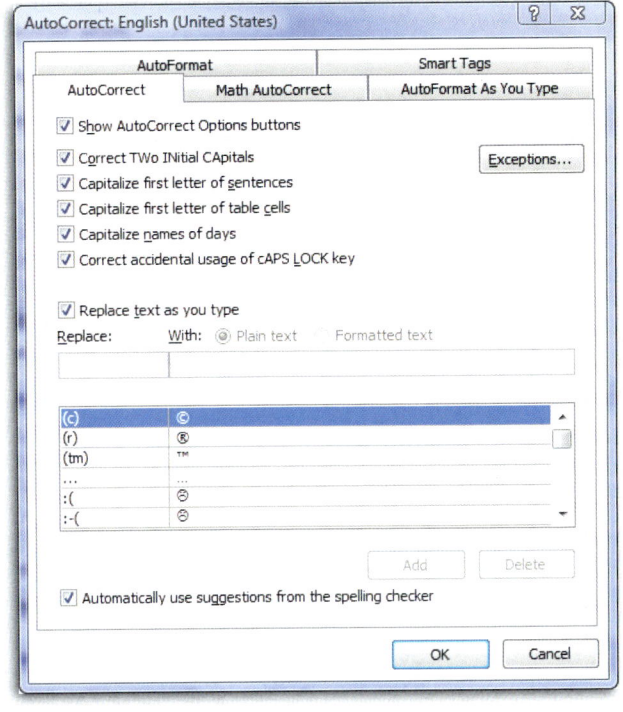

- **Capitalize First Letter of Sentences**: AutoCorrect will capitalize the first letter of the first word that comes at the beginning of a paragraph or after a sentence-ending punctuation mark.

- **Capitalize First Letter of Table Cells**: AutoCorrect will capitalize the first letter of the first word in each table cell.

- **Capitalize Names of Days**: AutoCorrect will capitalize days of the week, such as Monday, Tuesday, etc.

- **Correct Accidental Usage of CAPS LOCK Key**: When this feature is enabled, AutoCorrect notices when you have left the Caps Lock on and will turn it off and correct the text that was accidentally capitalized.

Use AutoCorrect to Save Time and Prevent Errors   113

34 Use AutoCorrect to Save Time and Prevent Errors (continued)

Changing or Removing an AutoCorrect Entry

While AutoCorrect entries, in general, are useful and save you time, there are some settings that might actually work against you. For example, a frequent troublemaker is the AutoCorrect entry for the copyright symbol. Those who use (c) to represent anything other than the Copyright symbol are often frustrated by this auto-correction. To edit an entry:

1. Select the **Microsoft Office** button.

2. Select **Word Options**.

3. Click **Proofing**.

4. Click **AutoCorrect Options** button.

5. Scroll through the **Replace Text as You Type** list to locate entries to edit or delete.

6. When the entry appears in the **Replace** and **With** boxes, you can edit the text in either box to change the entry or click the **Delete** button to remove it completely.

accelerate

Hot Tip: To create exceptions for some of the features, click the **Exceptions** button. The **AutoCorrect Exceptions** dialog box opens. For each tab, **Add** and **Delete** to manage the list of exceptions.

Bright Idea: You can insert blocks of text that you type frequently by adding text to this dialog box. For example, if you frequently type EEOC for "Equal Employment Opportunity Commission," you might consider adding EEOC to the list. This can be a major time saver if you use a lot of acronyms or have large portions of text you can enter by typing in a shortcut.

35 Customize Spellcheck and Grammar Check Options

Difficulty: ●●○○

PROBLEM While working on Word projects, you are distracted by notations alerting you to spelling and grammar errors as you type. You want to monitor spelling and grammar in the document creation process.

SOLUTION Customize the spelling and grammar checker by selecting specific options to employ (or not) as Word checks document's spelling and grammar.

See Also: Create Custom Spellcheck Lists for Documents and Projects

Step-by-Step

1. Click the **Microsoft Office** button **A**.

2. Select **Word Options** **B**.

3. Click **Proofing** **C**.

4. Basic spelling options are found in the **When correcting spelling in Microsoft Office Programs** section **D**. These apply to all Office applications, such as Word, Excel, and PowerPoint.

5. To set options for Word only, review options in the **When correcting spelling and grammar in Word** section **E**:

    - **Check spelling as you type**: Turn this off to stop Word from checking spelling (and red-underlining words).

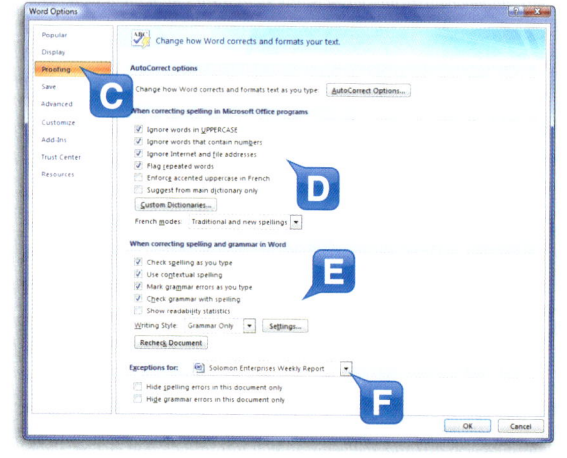

116   QuickClicks: Microsoft Word 2007

- **Use contextual spelling**: Turn this off to stop Word from blue-underlining words that might be used improperly in the current context.

- **Mark grammar errors as you type**: Turn this off to stop Word from checking grammar (green underlining words and phrases).

- **Recheck Document**: Click this button to run the spelling and grammar check again after changing the grammar settings to see if any additional errors or concerns are identified.

- **Show readability statistics**: Turn this on to display a box with readability information at the end of a spelling and grammar check with the Spelling and Grammar dialog box.

- **Writing Style**: Set the level of grammar check you require. Elect to check grammar only or to include other style issues such as contractions, commonly misspelled words, fragments, etc.

6. The **Exceptions for** section **F** allows you to select exceptions for any active document including the following.

   - **Hide spelling errors in this document only**: This does not turn off the spellchecking as you type. However, it prevents the red underlines from appearing on the screen.

   - **Hide grammar errors in this document only**: This does not turn off the grammar checking as you type. However, it prevents the green underlines from appearing on the screen.

35 Customize Spellcheck and Grammar Check Options (continued)

Grammar Settings

1. Select the **Microsoft Office** button.

2. Select **Word Options**.

3. Click **Proofing** G.

4. In the **When Correcting Spelling and Grammar in Word** section, click the **Settings** button H.

5. In the **Grammar Settings** dialog box, open the **Writing style** list and select the writing style to customize (Grammar only or Grammar & Style).

   - **Comma required before last list item**: When you have three or more items in a list, some writing styles prescribe a comma between the last two. However, in other writing styles, the comma is omitted. Choices are either *Always* or *Never*.

   - **Punctuation required with quotes**: Some writing styles prescribe that punctuation should fall within the quotation mark when both occur at the end of a sentence. In other writing styles, the punctuation falls outside of the quotes. Choices are *Don't Check*, *Inside*, or *Outside*. Inside is most commonly used.

   - **Spaces required between sentences**: Some writing styles prescribe one blank space between sentences while others prescribe two. Options are *one* or *two*.

118   QuickClicks: Microsoft Word 2007

Custom Spelling Dictionaries

You cannot edit the main dictionary in Word. Custom dictionaries are available for you to add and store words. To manage custom dictionaries:

1. Select the **Microsoft Office** button.
2. Select **Word Options**.
3. Click **Proofing**.
4. Click **Custom Dictionaries** **1**.
5. Select a custom dictionary from the list or add a new one.
6. In this **Custom Dictionaries** dialog box, you can edit word lists, adding to and/or deleting words from a custom dictionary.
7. Click **OK** when finished.

36 Create Custom Spellcheck Lists for Documents and Projects

Difficulty: ●●●○

PROBLEM When creating Word documents, your name is flagged as a misspelled word.

SOLUTION Add your name to a custom dictionary so it is no longer flagged. Creating a custom dictionary permits you to edit the word list and add specific words. Terms added to the custom dictionary will not be flagged by the spellchecker in your Word 2007 projects.

> **What Microsoft Calls It:** Custom Dictionaries

Step-by-Step

1. Click the **Microsoft Office** button.

2. Select **Word Options**.

3. Click **Proofing** **A**.

4. Click **Custom Dictionaries** **B**.

5. Select a custom dictionary from the list or add a new one.

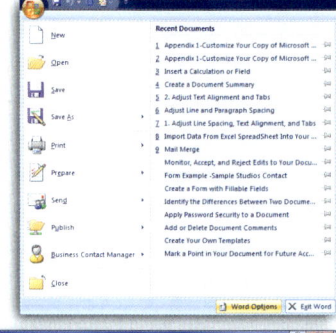

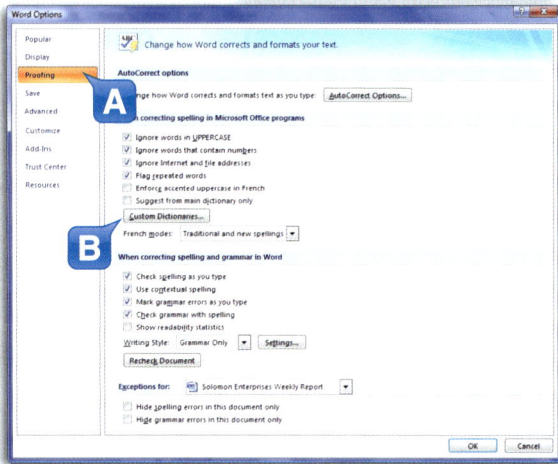

120 QuickClicks: Microsoft Word 2007

accelerate

6. Click **Edit Word List** C.

7. A dialog box appears listing all the words currently in that dictionary.

8. To add a new word, type it in the **Word(s)** box D and click **Add** E. ⚠️

9. To delete a word, select it and click **Delete**.

10. To clear the entire dictionary, click **Delete All**.

11. Click **OK** on all open dialog boxes when finished editing the custom dictionary.

Caution: Words can be no longer than 64 characters.

Hot Tip: You can create project-specific custom dictionaries. The more words you add to a dictionary, especially foreign words, names and acronyms, the more likely it is that a true typographical error will slip through the cracks. Creating custom dictionaries for each project can minimize the number of words added to any given list. This is especially useful for authors and those in legal professions.

Quickest Click: You can add an entire list of words at one time to a custom dictionary. This is useful when you have a list of frequently used terms, not included in the main dictionary—such as employee names, product names, or internal acronyms.

Create Custom Spellcheck Lists for Documents and Projects   121

37 Record and Play Back a Series of Actions

Difficulty: ●●○○

PROBLEM Every week a report is pulled from the tracking system and the information from the report needs to be translated into a summary document. The report, by default, displays the dollar currency symbol as the letter C. So, each week, you have to do a search and replace on hundreds of pages to edit this information.

SOLUTION Since you perform this manual action frequently, creating a macro would save time and money. A macro is a sequence of actions that Word will execute when you run it. Macros enable you to automate a variety of operations that typically would be completed manually.

> **What Microsoft Calls It:** Macros

Step-by-Step

Create a Macro

1. On the **View** tab **A**, in the **Macros** group, click the lower half of the **Macros** button **B**.

2. Select **Record Macro.**

122 QuickClicks: Microsoft Word 2007

accelerate

3. In the **Record Macro** dialog box, type a name for the macro C. The macro name must start with a letter and contain no spaces.

4. In the **Store macro in** box D, click the template or document from the dropdown box where you want to store the macro.

   • **All Documents**: Select this to have the macro available anytime you use Word.

   • **Documents Based On**: Select this to have the macro available anytime you use a document that is based on the current document.

   • **This Document**: Select this to have the macro available in the current document only.

5. In the **Description** box E, enter a description of the macro that will help you and others easily identify which actions the macro completes (optional).

6. **Assign macro to** a **Button** or **Keyboard** shortcut (optional).

7. Click the **OK** button to begin recording.

CONTINUE

Record and Play Back a Series of Actions   123

37 Record and Play Back a Series of Actions (continued)

8. The cursor changes from a mouse pointer to a recording symbol to indicate *Record Mode*. Word records both the keystrokes and the commands you choose from the ribbon.

   Note: You must use keyboard commands to move the cursor or select text in Record Mode. The mouse only clicks on commands and options. See Appendix F for Keyboard Shortcuts.

9. To stop recording actions, click **Stop Recording** on the **Macros** button, in the **Macros** group, on the **View** tab. Or click the stop button (blue box) on the task bar at the bottom left corner of the screen.

Run a Macro

1. On the **View** tab, in the **Macros** group, click **Macros**.

2. Click **View Macros**.

3. Click **Run**.

   Note: If you assigned the macro a shortcut when it was created, the macro can be run from the Quick Access Toolbar or the assigned keyboard shortcut.

Bright Idea: There are additional macro options available through the **Developer** tab in the **Code** group. To activate the **Developer** tab, click the **Microsoft Office** button and select **Word Options**. Select the **Show Developer tab in Ribbon** checkbox. Click the **OK** button.

Option: You can also use the macro controls on the left side of the task bar to start and stop your recording session.

start   stop

Record and Play Back a Series of Actions

38 Apply Password Security to a Document

Difficulty: ●●○○

PROBLEM You have created a report that needs to be sent to a Review Committee. Many of the committee members have assistants with access to their mailboxes, but you only want the confidential report to be viewed or changed by the members themselves.

SOLUTION You can assign a password and activate other security options so that only those with appropriate permissions can open the document.

When you password-protect a document, Word encrypts it. This password protection does not just stop the file from being opened without a password, but it physically changes the file. When you password-protect the file against changes, it simply prevents the file from being saved, unless the user has the password. For maximum security, set both passwords.

See Also: Create Templates

> **What Microsoft Calls It:** Protect Document

Step-by-Step

Prevent Unauthorized Readers from Opening a Document

1. Click the **Microsoft Office** button.
2. Select **Save As**.
3. In the **Save As** dialog box, click **Tools** **A**.
4. Choose **General Options** **B**.

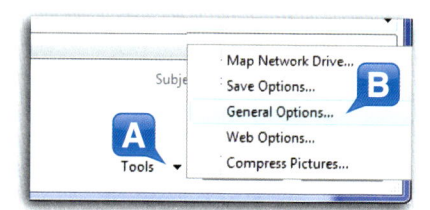

126   QuickClicks: Microsoft Word 2007

collaborate

5. In the **General Options** dialog box, select and type a password to open document **C**.

6. In the **Password to Modify** box, type a different password **D**.

   Note: You can use one or both passwords, but if you use both, they cannot be the same password.

7. Click **OK** **E**.

8. Confirm password(s) by re-typing it/them when prompted.

9. Click **OK**.

10. In the **Save As** dialog box, click **Save** to save the file with the password(s). ⚠️💡🔥

Change or Remove the Password Protection

1. Click the **Microsoft Office** button.

2. Click **Open** and browse to find the password-protected file.

3. Click **Open**.

4. Type the password in the **Password** dialog box **F**.

5. Click **OK** **G**.

6. If prompted, type another password, and click **OK**.

7. Click the **Microsoft Office** button and select **Save As**.

8. In the **Save As** dialog box, click **Tools**.

9. Choose **General Options**.

CONTINUE

Apply Password Security to a Document   **127**

38 Apply Password Security to a Document (continued)

10. In the **General Options** dialog box, select and type a new password or delete the password so the password text boxes are empty.

11. Click **OK** to apply changes.

12. Click **Save** and then **Yes** to replace existing document.

Restrict Formatting and Editing

1. Open the document you want to protect.

2. On the **Review** tab, in the **Protect** group, click **Protect Document**.

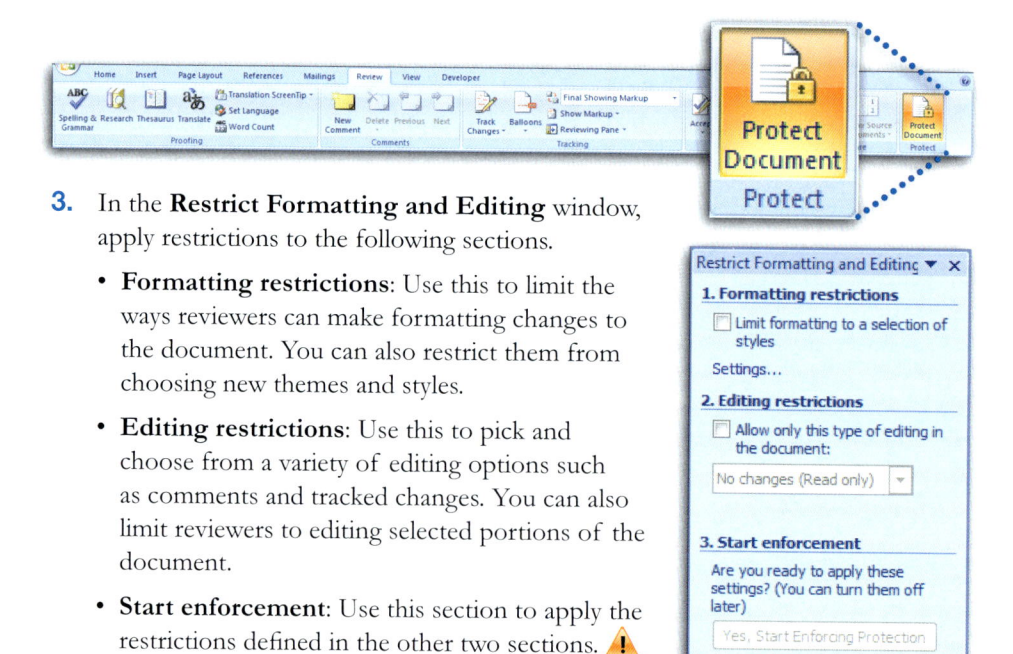

3. In the **Restrict Formatting and Editing** window, apply restrictions to the following sections.

   - **Formatting restrictions**: Use this to limit the ways reviewers can make formatting changes to the document. You can also restrict them from choosing new themes and styles.

   - **Editing restrictions**: Use this to pick and choose from a variety of editing options such as comments and tracked changes. You can also limit reviewers to editing selected portions of the document.

   - **Start enforcement**: Use this section to apply the restrictions defined in the other two sections.

128   QuickClicks: Microsoft Word 2007

collaborate

Caution: It is critical that you remember the password, as there is no way to retrieve the password if you forget it. This means that once protected, you cannot access the file without the password.

Bright Idea: You can password protect templates to keep those filling out your forms from making changes beyond the designated fields. If your computer is secure, you might consider keeping your copy protection-free and password protecting a second copy for distribution.

Hot Tip: For better security, a password should combine lowercase and uppercase letters, along with numbers and symbols.

Caution: If you do not password protect your document, users can still make changes to these formatting and editing restrictions by opening this window.

Apply Password Security to a Document

39 | Add, Respond to, and Delete Reviewer Comments

Difficulty: ●●○○

PROBLEM You have created a document and sent it to your coworkers for review. There are several sections of the document where you want your readers to make comments and/or respond to comments.

SOLUTION Comments in Word are like posting little notes onto the document. A document reviewer might insert a comment to ask the author a question or make a suggestion about a specific line of text. Word tracks which reviewer made which comment, allowing you to easily follow up on a comment, get more details, or provide a response to that particular reviewer.

See Also: Monitor, Accept, and Reject Edits to a Document; Appendix D–Track Changes and Comments Options

> **What Microsoft Calls It:** Document Comments

Step-by-Step

Reading or Editing Comments

Before you can read or review comments, you need to display them on the screen.

1. On the **Review** tab, click the **Show Markup** button and click **Comments**.

2. To click through comments, click the **Previous** or **Next** button.

3. To edit comments, click the text in the comment, make your changes, and then click outside the balloon to save it.

collaborate

Create a Comment

1. Select the text you want to comment on, or place the cursor at the position in the document where the comment should be inserted.

2. On the **Review** tab, in the **Comments** group, select **New Comment A**.

3. Type your comment in the balloon and then click outside the balloon to save it.

Add, Respond to, and Delete Reviewer Comments

39 Add, Respond to, and Delete Reviewer Comments (continued)

Respond to a Comment

1. Click the balloon of the comment.

2. On the **Review** tab, in the **Comments** group, select **New Comment**.

3. Type your response in the new comment balloon and then click outside the balloon to save it. 🔥

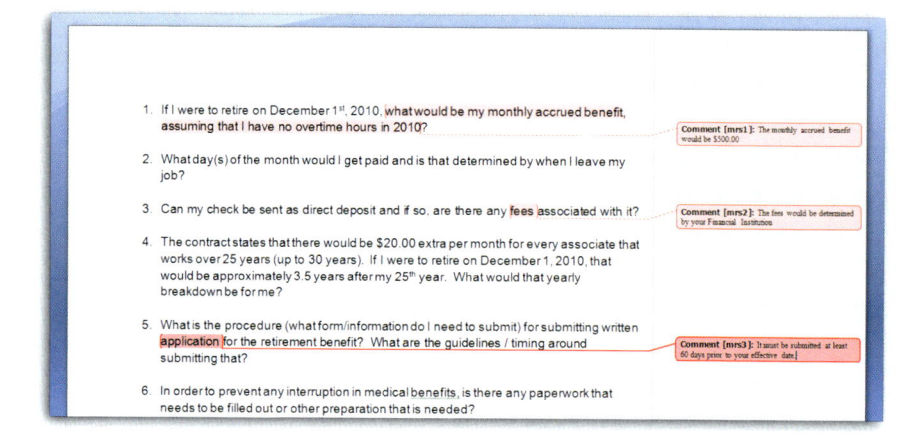

collaborate

Delete a Comment

1. Right-click the comment indicator in the text, or the comment body in the **Reviewing Pane**.

2. Select **Delete Comment** or click the **Delete Comment** button, in the **Comments** group, on the **Review** tab.

3. To delete all comments in a document, click the down arrow on the **Delete** button in the **Comments** group on the **Review** tab, and choose **Delete All Comments in Document**.

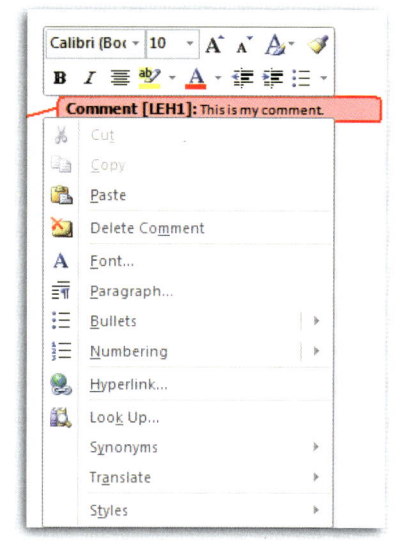

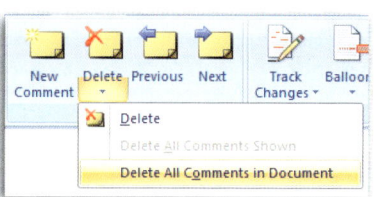

Hot Tip: Word will automatically move excess comments from the margin to the **Reviewing Pane**. The reviewing pane can sit on the side margin or bottom of the page. To use the reviewing pane to review comments, click the **Reviewing Pane** dropdown arrow on the **Review** tab. Click **Reviewing Pane Vertical** (for display on the side of the page) or **Reviewing Pane Horizontal** (for display at bottom of the page).

Add, Respond to, and Delete Reviewer Comments   133

40 Monitor, Accept, and Reject Edits to a Document

Difficulty: ●●○○

PROBLEM You created a report outlining the company's strategic priorities for the upcoming year. It included product, financial, and operational information. You sent it to the marketing director, the chief financial officer, and the V.P. of operations, as well as the head of Human Resources for review and comments. You enabled the track changes feature in the document and asked each to simply mark up the page and send it back to you. Now, you need to compile the information by either accepting or rejecting the edits.

SOLUTION The process of monitoring these edits starts by setting options before sending it out for review. When multiple people edit a document, it can be unclear who suggested what changes. This can be confusing. In order to track such data, Word provides several tools that enable users to mark up a document without permanently changing the original. This provides you the ability to monitor and accept or reject those recommended changes.

See Also: Add, Respond to, and Delete Reviewer Comments; Appendix D–Track Changes and Comments Options

What Microsoft Calls It: Track Changes

Step-by-Step

Set Track Changes Options

The Word default **Track Changes** options are useful for the basic user. However, to further customize these options for smarter editing, follow these steps:

1. On the **Review** tab, in the **Tracking** group, select **Track Changes** **A**.

2. Select **Change Tracking Options**.

134   QuickClicks: Microsoft Word 2007

collaborate

3. In the **Track Changes Options** dialog box B, specify the markup options you want when you make changes.

- **Insertions**: Marks inserted text.
- **Deletions**: Marks deleted text.
- **Formatting**: Marks formatting changes.
- **Changed Lines**: Sets the location of vertical line that marks changed paragraphs.
- **Comments Color**: Sets the color applied to all comments.

Monitor, Accept, and Reject Edits to a Document   135

40 Monitor, Accept, and Reject Edits to a Document (continued)

4. Specify the balloons options you want to use.

    - **Use Balloons (Print and Web Layout)**: Sets display option for balloons.
    - **Preferred Width**: Sets balloon width.
    - **Margin**: Sets margin location for balloons.

5. Click **OK** to apply any changes. 🔥

136 QuickClicks: Microsoft Word 2007

collaborate

Track, Accept and/or Reject Changes

1. On the **Review** tab, in the **Tracking** group, select **Track Changes**.

2. After reviews are complete, respond to the review marks by either accepting or rejecting each change individually or by accepting or rejecting all changes.

3. To accept changes, select **Accept** **C**.

4. Select either **Accept and Move to Next** or **Accept All Changes in Document**.

5. To reject changes, select **Reject** **D**.

6. Select either **Reject and Move to Next** or **Reject All Changes in Document**.

> **Hot Tip:** If you specify any of the colors in the dialog box as *By author,* Word will automatically assign a different color to each person's changes and comments. Word determines if a new person is editing the document by looking at the User Name set up in Word. This is especially useful when you have multiple editors.

41 | Identify the Difference between Two Documents

Difficulty: ●●○○

PROBLEM You are working on a project with your coworkers. You send out a draft for everyone to review and provide feedback. Each of your coworkers, one at a time, begins sending their versions back to you. You have to incorporate everyone's suggestions and changes into a master document.

SOLUTION If you want to compare multiple versions of a document and create one master copy, you can compare and merge these documents using Word 2007. The changes can be automatically merged into one document or viewed for comparison. When you compare or merge documents, the text that differs between the two versions will be highlighted in a different color or with tracking marks.

> **What Microsoft Calls It:** Compare and Combine Documents

Step-by-Step

Viewing Two Documents Side by Side

1. Open both documents.

2. Display one of the two as the active document.

3. On the **View** tab, in the **Window** group, click **View Side by Side** **A**.

   Note: If only two documents are open, Word will automatically place them side by side. If more than two are open, the **Compare Side by Side** *dialog box opens. Select the document to compare and click OK.*

138 QuickClicks: Microsoft Word 2007

collaborate

4. The two windows are set for synchronized scrolling.

5. This allows you to compare the documents line by line.

   Note: To turn off synchronized scrolling, click the Synchronized Scrolling button, in the Window group, on the View tab.

Comparing and Combining Documents

Combine merges the revisions from both copies into a single document, which can be either the original or the copy, as you specify, or a brand-new document. You can repeat the combine operation to combine revisions from multiple copies. All unique revision marks are kept in both copies. **Compare** generates a new copy that combines the two versions, and the revision marks are now combined and not attributable to specific reviewers.

1. On the **Review** tab, in the **Compare** group, click **Compare** **B**.

2. Click **Combine** from the menu **C**.

3. In the **Combine Documents** dialog box, select the original document from the **Original Document** dropdown menu **D**.

4. Open the **Revised Document** dropdown menu and select the other document to combine **E**.

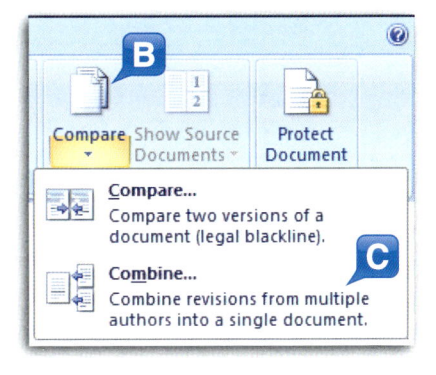

5. By default, the **Label Unmarked Changes With** setting is whatever user name is set up in Word as the current user. This can be edited.

Identify the Difference between Two Documents   139

41 Identify the Difference between Two Documents (continued)

6. Click the **More** button [F] to set additional options:

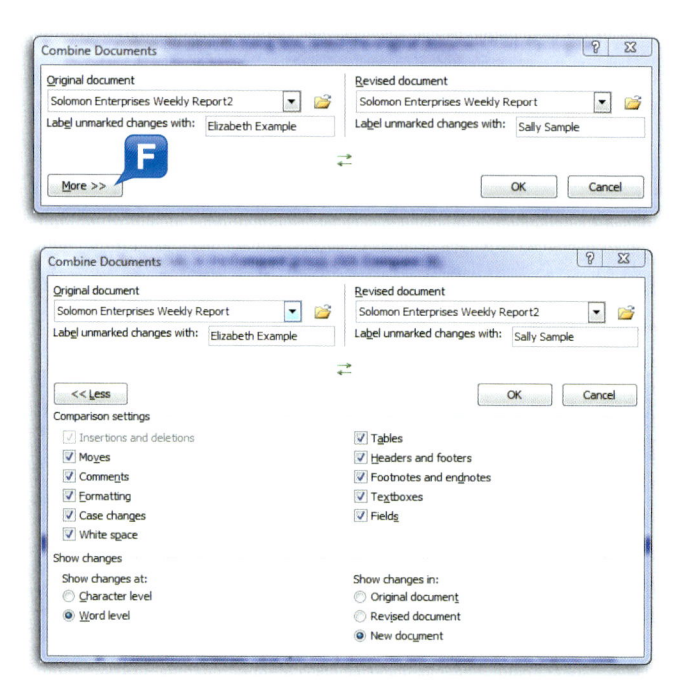

- **Comparison Settings**: Clear the check boxes for any comparisons you want to omit.

- **Show Changes At**: By default, revisions are marked at the Word level, but you can set this to Character level if you prefer.

- **Show Changes In**: Choose where the combined markup will appear. You can choose to place the revisions in the **Original document**, the **Revised document**, or a new document.

7. Click **OK** to combine the documents.

collaborate

- Original document
- Revised document
- Revision history
- Combined document
- Original document
- Revised document

Identify the Difference between Two Documents   141

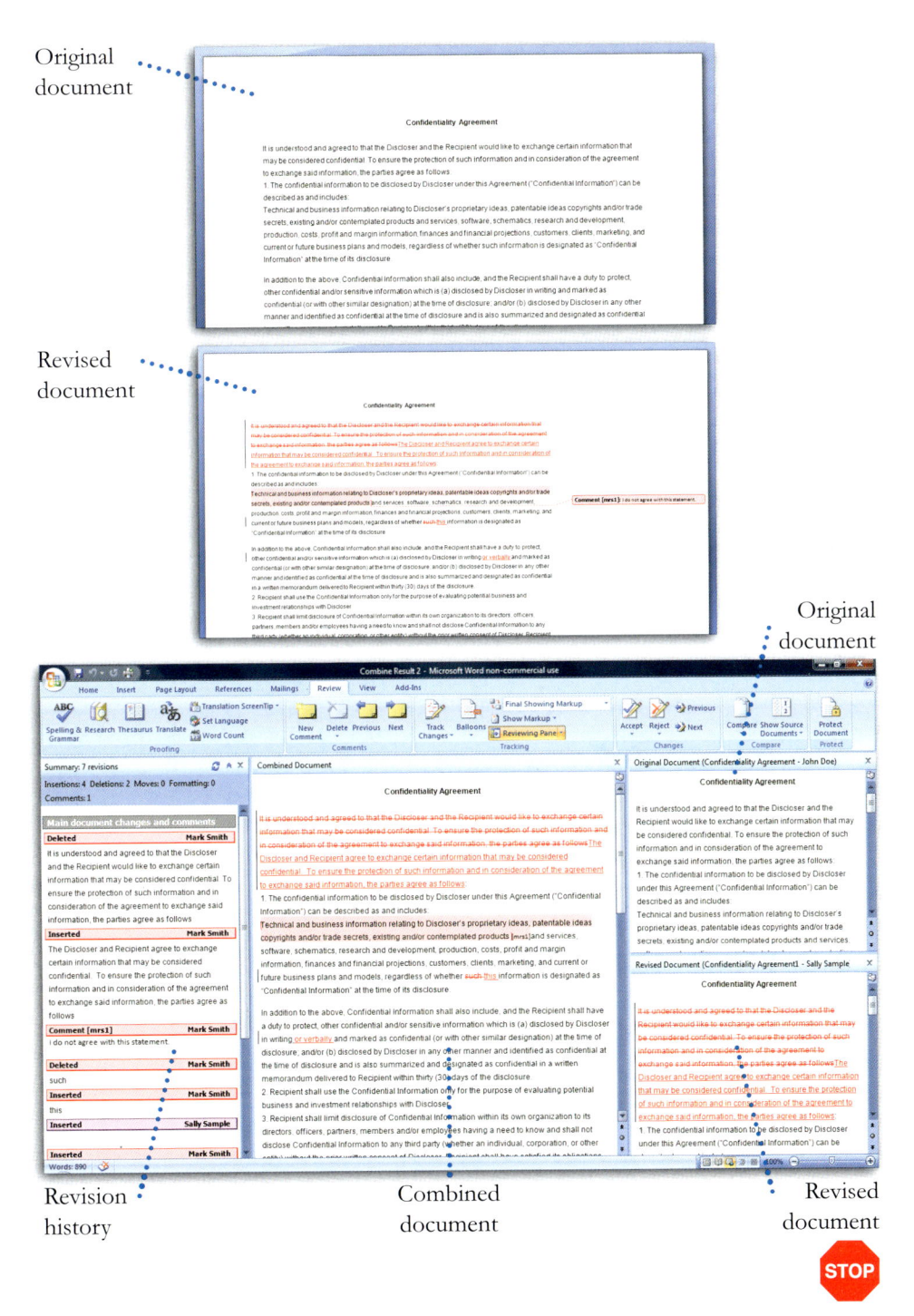

42 Import Data from an Excel Spreadsheet into a Document

Difficulty: ●●○○

PROBLEM You maintain a customer contact list in Excel. You are currently producing a memo to go out to all regional managers. The memo includes a variety of information—all text. You want to include the data from Excel in the spreadsheet without having to recreate the table.

SOLUTION Import the data from Excel and then format and sort it right in your Word document.

What Microsoft Calls It: Insert Objects

Step-by-Step

1. Place the cursor in the position where the Excel spreadsheet will be inserted.

2. On the **Insert** tab, in the **Text** group, select **Object** A.

3. Select **Create From File** tab B.

4. Click **Browse** C to select the location and select the file to include in the document.

5. Click **OK** D.

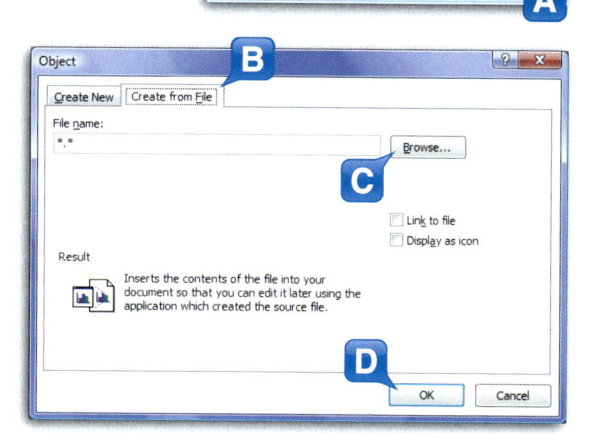

142   QuickClicks: Microsoft Word 2007

collaborate

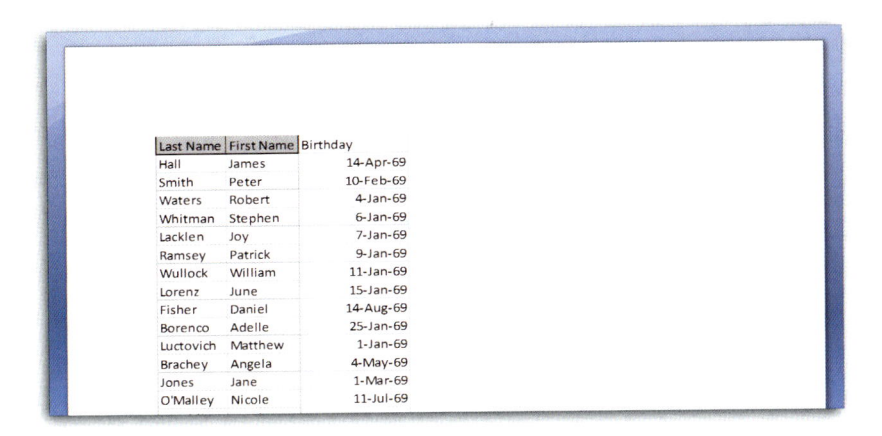

Last Name	First Name	Birthday
Hall	James	14-Apr-69
Smith	Peter	10-Feb-69
Waters	Robert	4-Jan-69
Whitman	Stephen	6-Jan-69
Lacklen	Joy	7-Jan-69
Ramsey	Patrick	9-Jan-69
Wullock	William	11-Jan-69
Lorenz	June	15-Jan-69
Fisher	Daniel	14-Aug-69
Borenco	Adelle	25-Jan-69
Luctovich	Matthew	1-Jan-69
Brachey	Angela	4-May-69
Jones	Jane	1-Mar-69
O'Malley	Nicole	11-Jul-69

Bright Idea: You can insert a blank Excel spreadsheet into an existing word document. This allows for data manipulation that a Word table does not allow, such as flexibility in sorting, formatting, and formulas/functions. On the **Insert** tab, in the **Text** group, select **Object**. In the **Create New** tab, select an Excel spreadsheet in the format you desire. Click **OK**.

Import Data from an Excel Spreadsheet into a Document   143

43 Use Data from an Excel Spreadsheet to Populate Fields in a Document

Difficulty: ●●○○

PROBLEM You have a student list created in Excel that contains all students' names and home addresses. You want to send a brochure advertising your new classes for the quarter.

SOLUTION You can use the Mail Merge function to pull the data you need from your existing Excel spreadsheet and create your envelopes for printing within minutes without having to retype any information. Mail Merge is great for letters, e-mail messages, envelopes, and labels. Word can pull data from a variety of source types. This is especially useful if you have an existing data source with the information you need.

> **What Microsoft Calls It:** Mail Merge

Step-by-Step

To Start Mail Merge

1. Click **Start Mail Merge** on the **Start Mail Merge** A group in the **Mailings** tab.

2. Select **Step by Step Mail Merge Wizard** to begin setting up your document B.

3. The **Mail Merge** task pane opens on the right side of your document.

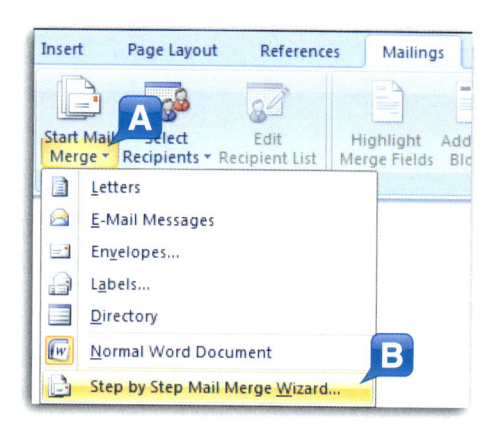

144   QuickClicks: Microsoft Word 2007

collaborate

4. Select what type of document you want to use **C**.

5. Edit options for your document. These options will change based upon the type of document you select.

6. In the **Select Recipients** task pane (step 3 of 6 in the Mail Merge task pane), click the **Browse** button to select the Excel file you want to pull from.

7. Once you have selected the file, the **Mail Merge Recipients** dialog box opens and displays the recipients that will be included in the mail merge. You can edit this list or click **OK** to continue.

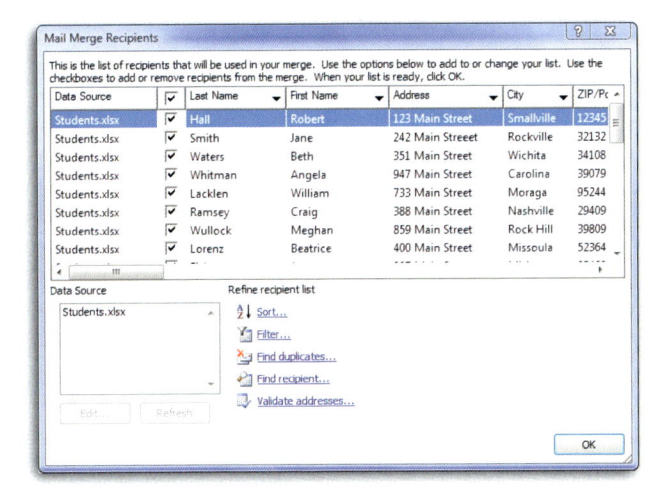

Use Data from an Excel Spreadsheet to Populate Fields in a Document   145

43 Use Data from an Excel Spreadsheet to Populate Fields in a Document (continued)

8. Click **Next** to move to the next step in the process and create the setup for your document. This might include actions like writing your letter (for a letter document) or arranging your envelope text.

9. Click **Next** to **Preview** (if applicable) your document.

10. Click **Next** to **Complete the Merge**.

collaborate

Bright Idea: You can create merge fields in any document. In addition to the traditional address labels and envelopes, this feature can be used to produce certificates, personalized letters, invitations, product labels, nametags, seating cards, advertising flyers, marketing collateral, retail item placards, newsletters—you name it!

Quickest Click: You can set up the main document manually. Create a new or existing document, click the **Mailings** tab, click the **Start Mail Merge** button, select a document type (letter, e-mail, envelopes, etc.), and then select any options, if prompted.

Quickest Click: You can connect the document to the source manually. Click the **Mailings** tab, click the **Select Recipients** button, and then select the data source you want and any related options if prompted.

44 Create a PowerPoint Presentation from a Word Document

Difficulty: ●●●○

PROBLEM The head of the department just informed you that you need to create a PowerPoint presentation using the data from your Monthly Overview Report to present to the executive team in three hours.

SOLUTION You can create a Microsoft PowerPoint presentation from an existing Word document. The Word document should be structured like an outline, using the predesigned heading styles in Word. PowerPoint uses these heading styles in the Word document to format the titles of each slide. For example, text formatted with the Heading 1 style becomes the title of a new slide. Text formatted with Heading 2 becomes the first level of text. This process will continue for all data formatted in this manner.

See Also: Create a Bulleted or Numbered List; Apply Styles to Text

Step-by-Step

1. Create a Word outline.

2. Select each slide title and assign it as Heading 1 **A**.

3. Select each sub-heading and assign it as Heading 2 **B**.

The Toys **A**
- New Products
- Tools of the Trade
- A Picture Is Worth 1000 Words
- Making a Smooth Transition
- Saving the Day
- It's SHOWTIME!

B

The "Elves"
- New Hires **A**
- Reorganization

148 QuickClicks: Microsoft Word 2007

collaborate

4. Save the document and close it.

5. Open **PowerPoint** and create a new presentation.

6. Add a new slide after the title slide.

7. On that new slide, click the dropdown arrow at the bottom of the **New Slide** button and select **Slides from Outline**.

8. Browse to your Word file and select it.

9. Click the **Open** button.

Hot Tip: To save time formatting, decide what theme you want to use in the PowerPoint Slide Show. Use that same theme when you assign the heading styles to your outline in Word, as the selected style carries over into PowerPoint when you import the outline to the slides.

Create a PowerPoint Presentation from a Word Document   149

45 | Create a Form with Fillable Fields

Difficulty: ●●●○

PROBLEM You want to do a widespread survey through e-mail of your customers to get updates on contact information, as well as provide customers with an opportunity to make comments on service or products.

SOLUTION You can create a form in Word to e-mail to your customer group. With fillable fields, the form can be very quick and easy for the customers to complete and return. Forms enable you to gather information using fill-in-the-blank fields. Form fields (such as text, picture, list boxes, and date pickers) are called **Content Controls** in Word 2007. Using forms in Microsoft Word is a great option for those who do not have the technical skill or platform to create web forms. Forms created in Word can be printed and completed on paper or filled out from within Word.

See Also: Perform Calculations in a Table; Create Templates; Add a Table to a Document; Format Table Borders, Layout, and Shading; Apply Borders and Shading to Text or a Page; Apply Password Security to a Document

> **What Microsoft Calls It:** Content Controls, Legacy Controls, ActiveX Controls

Step-by-Step

Enable the Developer Tab

The **Developer** tab is required to create **Content Controls** in Word. If you don't see the **Developer** tab on your ribbon, you need to enable it.

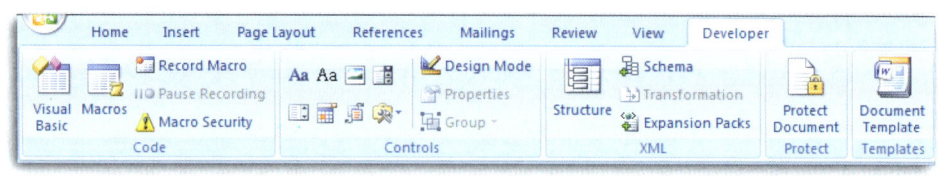

150 QuickClicks: Microsoft Word 2007

collaborate

1. Click the **Microsoft Office** button **A**.

2. Select **Word Options** **B**.

3. Select **Popular** **C**.

4. Click **Show Developer tab in the Ribbon** **D**.

5. Click **OK** **E**.

Form Layout

Design the layout of your form. Many authors elect to use tables to create the form layout or design. Using tables helps to line up the text, instructions, or labels for **Content Controls** in an organized manner. By using a table for the layout, you can add borders and/or shading for a more artistic presentation, or you may elect to use no borders or shading for a clean look. Or you may opt for other formatting, such as adding multiple columns to a page. This is an individual design preference. For this example, a table was created and all text was added in preparation for inserting the **Content Controls**.

Create a Form with Fillable Fields   151

45 Create a Form with Fillable Fields (continued)

Adding the Form Fields (Content Controls)

After you have finished designing the form, add the form fields—called **Content Controls**. These controls are where those filling out the form insert their information. **Content Controls**, located on the **Developer** tab in the **Controls** group, include **Text** boxes, **Images**, **Dropdown** menus, **Dates**, and **Legacy Tools**.

1. Place your cursor in the position where you want to add a form field **F**.

2. Hover over the graphic icons in the **Controls** group on the **Developer** tab to see the text describing each control **G**.

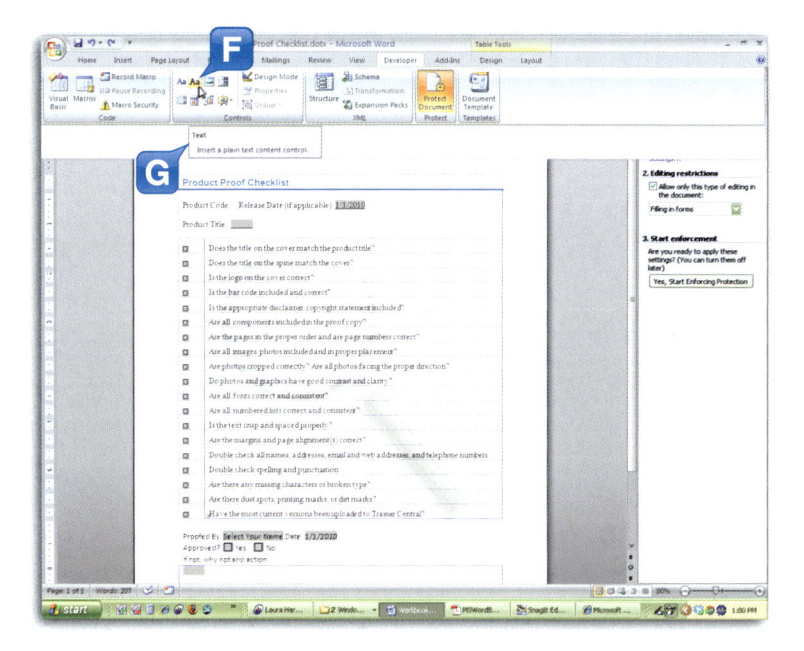

3. Select the control you want to insert into your form.

152   QuickClicks: Microsoft Word 2007

collaborate

4. Repeat these steps for each **Content Control**.

   - **Rich Text** Aa : Text boxes that hold a paragraph of formatted text. This is useful where you need to fill in information. The Rich Text control allows users typing in the information to format the text within the box to their specifications. For example, they can type in their information and italicize or bold a certain word. Or they can change the color of the font on their entry.

   - **Text** Aa : Use the plain Text box for most forms. The advantage of these controls is that they can hold more than one paragraph. Rich text controls only allow one paragraph.

   - **Picture** : This control feature allows images to be inserted, such as photos, logos, charts, etc.

   - **Combo Box** : This control feature displays a list of options and includes a text box for entries that do not appear on the list. Use a combo box to provide "suggested" options, but still allow users to enter their own information.

   - **Dropdown List** : This provides users a dropdown menu that limits the options users can choose from. This is especially useful when you want a user to choose only one of the options, such as Yes/No, or from which city or state they reside. This also eliminates spelling errors or typos that could lead to errors.

   - **Date Picker** : This is a calendar tool that lets users easily select a date.

   - **Building Block Gallery** : Building blocks are predesigned, preformatted chunks of text, pictures, and other content that people can insert into documents.

   - **Legacy Tools** : These are controls and form fields used in previous versions of Word. These do not have the same functionality as the new content controls, and are primarily used only to edit a form that was developed in a previous version of Word.

   Note: Check boxes and radio buttons are only available in Legacy Tools.

CONTINUE

Create a Form with Fillable Fields   **153**

Create a Form with Fillable Fields (continued)

Setting Properties for Content Controls

Content Controls can be locked so that users cannot delete or edit the contents.

1. Click the **Design Mode** button, in the **Controls** group, on the **Developer** tab.

2. Click on the individual **Content Control** within the form whose properties you want to edit.

3. Right-click and select **Properties** from the menu. Each **Content Control** has slightly different property values available.

- **Title**: Appears in your document on the content control tab. If you do not apply a title, Word leaves the tab and the title field blank.

- **Tag**: Used by other computer programs to identify and then read or write to the contents in your control.

- **Content control cannot be deleted**: Check this box to protect the field from being deleted by users.

- **Content control cannot be edited**: Check this box to protect the control from being edited by users. This is useful if you want to display the information in the control without users being able to edit. This can be useful in other types of documents as well.

- **Allow carriage returns (multiple paragraphs)**: Check this box to allow users to put several paragraphs in a **Text** control.

- **Remove content control when contents are edited**: Check this box to create a prompt for the document. Once a user types in text, the content control disappears and the text takes its place.

- **Dropdown List Properties**: Both the **Combo Box** and the **Dropdown** list content controls contain properties where you provide words and options for the lists.

- **Display the date like this**: This is a property field in the **Date Picker**. This is where you choose the format for the date (i.e., January 12, 2010 vs 1/12/10).

- **Locale and Calendar type**: These are property fields used in the **Date Picker**. These are used to control the way dates are shown in different regions and languages.

collaborate

- **Store XML contents in the following format when mapped**: This option is used in the Date Picker control to communicate date information to other programs.

- **Gallery** and **Category**: These options are used in the **Building Block Gallery** control to select specific building blocks that can be inserted into the document.

Protect Your Form

1. Click **Protect Document**, in the **Protect** group, on the **Developer** tab.

2. The **Restrictions Pane** opens on the right side of the document. Under **Editing Restrictions**, check **Allow Only** and then choose **Filling in Forms**.

3. Click **Yes, Start Enforcing Protection**.

4. You will be prompted to enter a password. You do not have to enter a password to protect the document, but without the password, users will be able to turn off the protection and modify the form.

Caution: If you choose to enter a password, be sure to remember it, as Word cannot retrieve it.

Hot Tip: To turn off protection, click **Protect Document** again, and click the **Stop Protection** button.

Create a Form with Fillable Fields   155

APPENDICES

A Customize Your Copy of Microsoft Word

The **Word Options** dialog box allows you to customize your copy of Microsoft Word to create specifications that make it easier for you to work, based on your preferences.

To access the Word Options dialog box:

1. Click the **Microsoft Office** button.

2. Click **Word Options**.

3. The **Word Options** dialog box opens.

Defining Shortcut Keys

Customize keyboard shortcuts so you can perform your favorite commands by using quick keyboard strokes.

1. In the **Word Options** dialog box, click **Customize** ▪A▪.

2. At the bottom of the box, click the **Customize** button ▪B▪ next to **Keyboard shortcuts**.

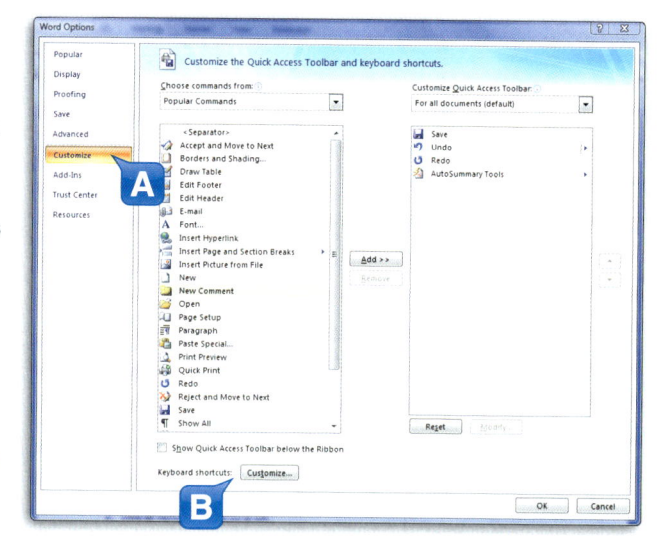

3. The **Customize Keyboard** dialog box opens. It offers several lists, text boxes, and buttons. At the top, two list boxes labeled **Categories** and **Commands** are available.

4. On the left, choose from the **Categories** options to show commands in the **Commands** box on the right.

   Note: When you make a selection in the Categories box, it changes the commands shown in the Commands box. For example, if you use tables frequently and want to assign a shortcut to the command to insert a table into your document, choose the Insert Tab in the Categories text box. The Commands box on the right then displays a list of commands related to inserting objects into your document.

158   QuickClicks: Microsoft Word 2007

appendices

5. In the **Commands** list, select the command you want to create a shortcut for.

6. Below the **Commands**, in the **Press new shortcut key** box, type the keys for your new shortcut. When you press keys on our keyboard, Word records them in the **Current keys** box on the left. You can use the **Alt**, **Shift**, and **CTRL** keys in combination with other keys. If you press them without another key, nothing will happen. 🔥

7. Below the **Current keys** box, review the **Currently assigned to** text box to make sure that the shortcut is correct and does not conflict with another shortcut that you already use.

8. In the **Save changes in** box, choose where to save the keyboard shortcut.

9. Click **Assign** to save the keyboard shortcut.

10. Click the **Close** button to close the **Customize Keyboard** box.

11. Click **OK** to close the **Word Options** box.

Setting Popular Word Options

Since every person could use Word in a slightly different way, **Word Options** allows you to change popular options to personalize what appears in the Word window. When you change these options, Word uses them for all Word windows you open, unless you change them.

1. In the **Word Options** dialog box, click **Popular**.

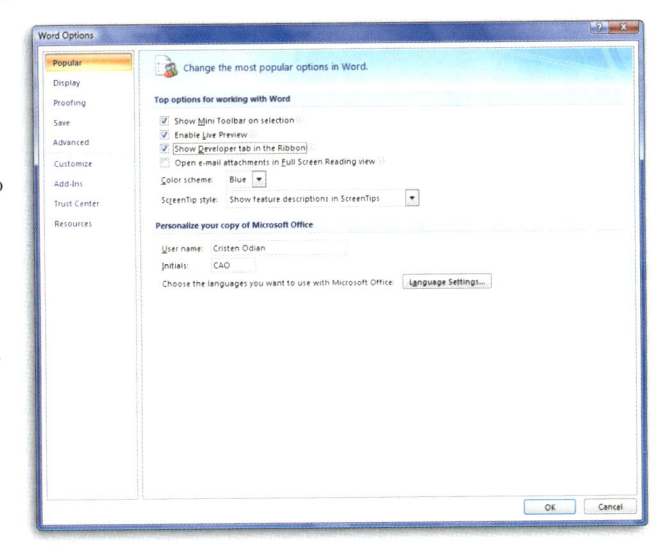

Appendix A: Customize Your Copy of Microsoft Word   **159**

Customize Your Copy of Microsoft Word (continued)

2. Select the **Top options for working with Word** you want.

   - **Show Mini Toolbar on Selection**: Select this option to show a miniature semi-transparent toolbar that helps you work with selected text.

   - **Enable Live Preview**: Select this option to show preview changes in a document.

   - **Show Developer Tab in the Ribbon**: Select this option to access developer controls, write code, or create macros.

   - **Open E-mail Attachments in the Full Screen Reading View**: Select this option to use Full Screen Reading view or clear to use Print Layout view.

   - **Color Scheme**: Click the dropdown arrow to select a Windows-related color scheme.

   - **ScreenTip style**: Click the down arrow to select a screen tip option:
     - Show enhanced ScreenTips
     - Don't show enhanced ScreenTips
     - Don't show ScreenTips

3. Type your name and initials as you want them to appear in **Properties** and **Comments** that you insert into documents.

4. Click **OK** to close window and apply changes.

appendices

Change Page Display Options

1. In the **Word Options** dialog box, click **Display**.

2. Select or clear any of the check boxes to change the display options you want.

   - **Show white space between pages in Print Layout view**: Select this option to display top and bottom margins.

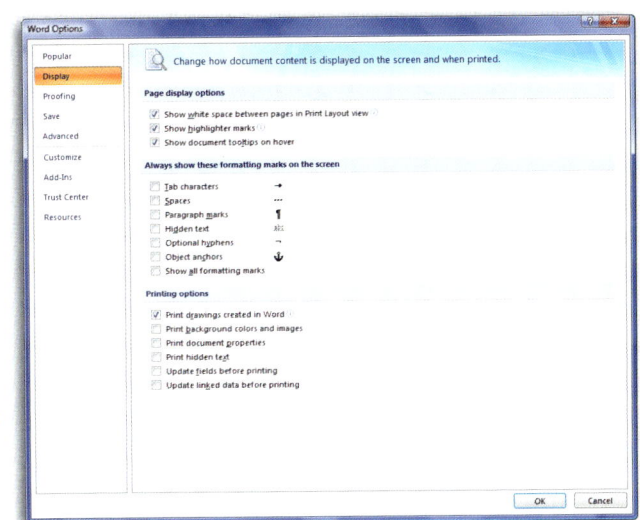

   - **Show highlighter marks**: Select this option to display highlighted text on the screen and in print.

   - **Show document tooltips on hover**: Select this option to display information when you point to a hyperlink or reviewer's comment.

3. Select or clear any of the check boxes to display or hide the formatting marks you want.

   - Tab characters, Spaces, Paragraph marks, Hidden text, Optional hyphens, or Object anchors.

   - Show all formatting marks.

4. Click OK to close window and apply changes.

> **Hot Tip**: If you make a mistake in selecting your shortcut, use the **Backspace** button on your keyboard to remove it. The **Delete** key does not work, since it is considered one of the keystrokes. If you hit the **Delete** key, "Del" appears in the text box.

Appendix A: Customize Your Copy of Microsoft Word   161

B Save a Document to the Appropriate File Format

Users can select from a wide variety of file formats to save a Word 2007 document. Choosing the appropriate file format depends upon the technological specifications of the users of the document. It is important to know how a document will be used– who will view or edit the document, and how often it will be changed. See table below for name and description of the different available file formats.

Format	Extension	Description
Word Document	.docx	The default format for Word 2007.
Word Macro-Enabled Document	.docm	A Word document that supports macro usage. * The new .docx format does not support macros for security reasons.
Word 97-2003	.doc	A backward compatible document format for users still working with an older version of Word.
Word Template	.dotx	The Word 2007 format for templates.
Word Macro-Enabled Template	.dotm	Macros can be stored in this template format. * The .dotx format does not support macros for security reasons.
Word 97-2003 Template	.dot	A backward compatible template format for users still working with an older version of Word.
Single-File Web Page	.mhtml or .mht	A web page where all graphics are embedded. Used to create HTML-based e-mail.
Web Page	.html or .htm	A web page that retains all the coding it needs for full use in Word, in addition to all coding needed for full use on the Web. Graphics and additional files are stored in a separate folder.
Web Page, Filtered	.html or .htm	A web page that contains only standards-compliant HTML code and no Word coding.

appendices

Format	Extension	Description
Rich Text Format	.rtf	A generic word processing format, supported by almost all word processing programs other than Word. Retains basic features as tables and text formatting.
Plain Text	.txt	This format saves the text only with no formatting.
Word XML Document	.sml	A document in eXtensible Markup Language, easily integrated with XML projects.
Word 2003 XML Document	.xml	A document in the Word 2003 version of XML.

Formatting Options

Margins

Margins are the blank spaces between the edge of a page and the text. The default setting for Word documents is 1.25 inches on the left and right and 1 inch on the top and bottom. You can use the mouse pointer to adjust margins visually for the entire document, or you can use the Page Setup dialog box to set exact measurements for either a portion or the entire document.

Adjusting Document Margins

1. On the **Page Layout** tab, in the **Page Setup** group, click **Margins**.

2. Select one of the preset margin options or click **Custom Margins**.

3. In the **Page Setup** dialog box, type new margin measurements in inches in the **Top**, **Bottom**, **Left**, or **Right** boxes and **Gutter** boxes.

4. Click the **Apply to** dropdown arrow and click **Selected Text**, **This Point Forward** or **Whole Document**.

5. To make new margin settings the default for all new Word documents, click **Default** and click **Yes**.

6. Click **OK** to apply settings.

Page Numbers

Add page numbers to your document by using the headers and footers.

1. On the **Insert** tab, in the **Header & Footer** group, click **Page Number**.

2. Select **Top of Page** or **Bottom of Page** and select a pre-formatted page number placement.

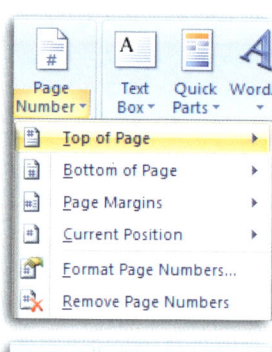

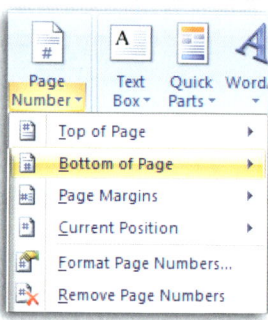

164   QuickClicks: Microsoft Word 2007

appendices

Styles

A style is a format-enhancing tool that includes font typefaces, font size, effects (bold, italics, underline, etc.), and colors.

Change Font Typeface and Size

1. Click the arrow next to the font name and select a font.   Calibri (Body)

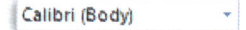

2. You can preview how the new font will look by highlighting the text and hovering over the new font typeface.

3. To change the font size, click the arrow next to the font size and select a size

    OR

4. Click the increase or decrease font size buttons.

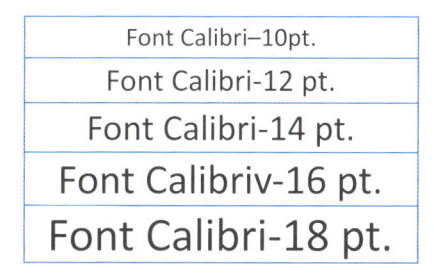

Font Calibri–10pt.
Font Calibri-12 pt.
Font Calibri-14 pt.
Font Calibriv-16 pt.
Font Calibri-18 pt.

Font Styles and Effects

1. Select the text and click the Font Styles included on the Font Group.
   - **Bold**
   - *Italicize*
   - Underline
   - ~~Strikeout~~
   - Subscript (H_2SO_4)
   - Superscript (Microsoft® Word®)
   - Change Case
     - Sentence case
     - Lowercase
     - UPPERCASE
     - Capitalize Each Word
     - tOGGLE cASE

Appendix C: Formatting Options   165

Formatting Options (continued)

Change Text Color

1. Select the text and click the **Colors** button in the **Font Group** **A**.

2. Select the color by clicking the down arrow next to the font color button.

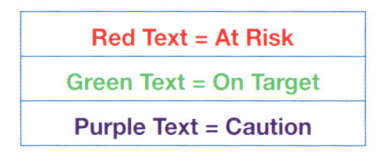

> Red Text = At Risk
> Green Text = On Target
> Purple Text = Caution

Highlight Text

1. Select the text and click the **Highlight** button, in the **Font** group, on the **Home** tab **B**.

2. To change the color of the highlighter, click the down arrow next to the highlight button.

166   QuickClicks: Microsoft Word 2007

appendices

Copy Formatting

1. Select the text with the formatting you want to copy.

2. Click the **Format Painter** button **C** in the **Clipboard** group on the **Home** tab.

3. Apply the copied format by selecting the text you want formatted.

Clear Formatting

Select the text from which you want to clear the formatting.

1. Click the **More Styles** dialog box **D** in the **Styles** group on the **Home** tab.

2. Click **Clear Formatting**.

Note: If you double-click the Format Painter button, you can select multiple areas of text to apply the formatting. To stop copying the formatting, click on the Format Painter button again.

> **Hot Tip: Gutters** allow for additional margin space so that all the document text remains visible after binding. To set the gutters for normal binding, display the **Margins** tab in the **Page Setup** dialog box. Click the **Multiple Pages** dropdown arrow and click **Book Fold**.

Appendix C: Formatting Options   167

D | Track Changes and Comments Options

Setting up Specs for Balloons Used for Comments

Option	Description
Preferred Width	The width of extra space that appears to the right of the page onscreen where the balloons appear.
Measure In	The unit of measurement for the preceding setting.
Margin	The side of the page where the balloons appear. This defaults to right.
Show Lines Connecting to Text	Connects a balloon to the comment or changes the balloon it refers to.
Paper Orientation in Printing	Auto: Switches to Landscape, if needed, to make comments fit. Preserve: Maintains page's established orientation Force Landscape: Always prints in landscape when comments are present.

appendices

Changing the Colors and Markings Used for Revisions

Option	Description
Insertions	New text, typically indicated by underlining and a different color. Your choices are Color Only, Bold, Italic, Underline, Double Underline, and Strikethrough.
Deletions	Deleted text, typically indicated by strikethrough and a different color. The choices are the same as for Insertions, plus a few additional, such as Hidden, ^, #, and double strikethrough.
Changed Lines	Any line in which there is a change, typically indicated by a vertical line at the border. The settings here are Left Border, Right Border, Outside Border and None.
Comments	Notes you insert with the New Comment feature. Set the color of the comment balloon or indicator.
Moves	Track moves from one location to another. Here you can select the same options as available for Insertions and Deletions.
Table Cell Highlighting	Changes you make to a table structure are marked by applying colors to the cells affected.
Formatting	Formatting is not tracked by default, but you can enable its tracking and choose what marks and colors are used.

D Track Changes and Comments Options (continued)

Views

When you are reviewing edits to your document, you can decide how the edited text will appear. To do so, make a selection from the **Display for Review** dropdown in the **Tracking** group of the **Review** tab.

Below are illustrations demonstrating what each view looks like for a single piece of marked-up text.

Original: This is what the document looked like before any changes were made.

Congratulations on your having purchased your very own copy of *QuickClicks: Microsoft Word 2007*. You have wisely invested in yourself and taken a huge steps forward with regards to your personal and perfessional development.

This reference guide is an important tool in your productive toolbox, allowing you to maximize your productivity by efficiently using the word processing featyres inherent to Microsoft Word. The tips in this reference guide are all written for the user who is in possession of a basic understanding of word processing functions and at least one year's experience using other Microsoft Office applications.

appendices

Original Showing Markup and Final Showing Markup: This is what the passage looks like when the edits are displayed. These views are almost always identical.

> Congratulations on your ~~having~~ purchas~~ed your very own copy~~ of *QuickClicks: Microsoft Word 2007*. You have ~~wisely~~ invested wisely in yourself and taken a ~~huge~~ step~~s~~ forward with regard~~s~~ to your personal and p<u>ro</u>er fessional development. ¶
>
> This reference guide is an important tool in your productiv~~ity~~<u>e</u> toolbox, allowing you to maximize your productivity by ~~efficiently~~ effectively using the word processing ~~featyres~~ functions ~~inherent to~~ within Microsoft Word. The tips in this reference guide are ~~all~~ written for the user ~~who is in possession of~~ with a basic understanding of word processing functions and at least one year~~'s~~ experience using other Microsoft Office applications. ¶

Final: This is what the document will look like after all edits are accepted.

> Congratulations on your purchase of *QuickClicks: Microsoft Word 2007*. You have invested wisely in yourself and taken a step forward with regard to your personal and professional development. ¶
>
> This reference guide is an important tool in your productivity toolbox, allowing you to maximize your productivity by effectively using the word processing functions within Microsoft Word. The tips in this reference guide are written for the user with a basic understanding of word processing functions and at least one year experience using other Microsoft Office applications. ¶

E | Create and Use Digital Signatures

Digital signatures are certifications of a document's authenticity. When sending important documents via e-mail or other online message service, a digital signature can provide some measure of certainty that a document has actually come from its alleged source and that it has not been altered since it was sent.

You can get a certificate from a certificate authority (a third party service online), but it is not free. To find out about third party certificates, choose **Office**, **Finish**, **Add a Digital Signature,** and then click **Signature Services** from the **Office Marketplace**. You can also self-certify a document, but this is not very secure and carries no legal authority. If you want to practice using digital signatures, though, a self-certificate will work.

Add a Digital Signature:

1. Click the **Microsoft Office** button.

2. Select **Prepare**.

3. Choose **Add a Digital Signature**.

4. If you do not have a third-party, digital signature file installed, a dialog box will offer to take you to **Office Marketplace** or to continue.

appendices

5. Click **OK** to continue.

6. In the **Get a Digital ID** dialog box, Microsoft will offer you options for obtaining a digital ID.

7. Follow the prompts to either create your own or use a third party to obtain the digital ID.

> **Caution:** If you are utilizing a digital signature for legal or organizational use, discuss your options with legal counsel to make sure that you are following proper procedure for liability purposes.

F Keyboard Shortcuts

A variety of keyboard shortcuts are available in Word and throughout Office 2007. The table below outlines some of the most common keyboard shortcuts.

Keyboard Shortcut	Description
ESC	Cancels an action
CTRL+Z	Undo the last action
CTRL+Y	Redo or repeat the last action
CTRL+SHFT+SPACEBAR	Create a non-breaking space
CTRL+B	Bold Text
CTRL+I	Italicize Text
CTRL+U	Underline Text
CTRL+SHFT+<	Decrease font size one value
CTRL+SHFT+>	Increase font size one value
CTRL+SPACEBAR	Remove paragraph or character formatting
CTRL+C	Copy selected text or object
CTRL+X	Cut selected text or object

appendices

Keyboard Shortcut	Description
CTRL+ALT+V	Paste special
CTRL+SHFT+V	Paste formatting only
CTRL+SHFT+G	Open the Word Count dialog box
CTRL+V	Paste text or object

Index

Symbols
3-D Format *45*
3-D Rotation *45*

A
Accept Changes *137*
ActiveX *150*
Align Left *6*
Alignment *6, 8, 68*
Align Right *7*
Arrange *10, 39, 41, 46, 47*
AutoCorrect *112, 113, 114, 115*
AutoSummary *90, 91*

B
Background *14, 28*
Bibliography *92, 94, 97, 98*
Bookmark *76, 78, 79, 80, 82, 86, 89*
Borders *14, 56, 59*
Bring Forward *47*
Bring to Front *47*
Building Block *64, 65*
Bullet *22, 23*
Bulleted List *21, 22, 23, 24*

C
Calculation *62*
Caption *50, 51*
Cell Height *56*
Center *6, 7*
Check Spelling as You Type *116*
Citations *94, 96, 97, 98*
Clear Formatting *167*
Clip Art *38, 42*
Column Break *10, 11, 12, 13*
Columns *11, 13*
Combine *138, 139*
Combo Box *153, 154*
Comments *91, 110, 128, 130, 131, 132, 133, 137, 168*
Compare *138, 139*

Content Controls *150, 151, 152, 153, 154*
Continuous Break *12*
Controls *150, 151, 152, 153, 154*
Convert Text to Table *55*
Crop *40, 41*
Cross Reference *78, 80, 87*
Custom Dictionaries *116, 119, 120, 121*

D
Date Picker *150, 153*
Developer Tab *125, 150*
Digital Signature *172*
Document Comments *130*
Document Summary *90*
Dropdown List *153*

E
Editing Restrictions *155*
Endnote *92, 93, 111*

F
Field *64, 104, 111, 144, 146, 150, 152, 154*
File Format *162*
Find *27, 49, 50, 82, 86, 108, 109, 110, 111, 127*
Find and Replace *108, 109, 110, 111*
Font *2, 3, 18, 21, 23, 26, 30, 35, 36, 61, 89, 109, 165, 166*
Footer *64, 68, 69, 70, 71, 72, 73, 164*
Footnote *92, 93, 98, 111*
Formula *62, 63, 143*

G
Grammar Check *116, 118*
Group *46, 47, 48, 49*
Gutters *164, 167*

H
Header *68, 70, 71, 72, 73, 164*
Highlight Text *166*
Hyperlink *74, 75, 76, 77, 78, 85*

index

I

Illustrations *38, 42, 50, 52*
Image *38, 40, 42, 44, 46, 48, 50, 70, 72, 152*
Image Style *44*
Index *86, 87, 88, 89*
In-Line References *96*
Insert Object *142*
Insert Row *58*

J

Justify *7*

K

Keyboard Shortcuts *158, 174*

L

Layer *46, 47*
Legacy Controls *150*
Line Color *44*
Line Spacing *2, 3*
Line Style *14, 44*

M

Macro *103, 105, 122, 123, 124, 125, 160, 162*
Mail Merge *144, 145, 147, 148*
Manual Page Break *66*
Margins *7, 21, 52, 68, 69, 70, 161, 164, 167*
Mark Grammar Errors as you Type *117*
Merge Cells *56, 58*
Multi-Level List *25*

N

Numbered List *22, 24, 25, 148*
Number Format *23, 63*

O

Office Button *90, 102, 104, 106, 112, 114, 116, 118, 119, 125, 126, 151, 158, 172*
Orphans *4*

Outline *24, 148*

P

Page Break *4, 5, 66*
Page Numbers *68, 87, 164*
Paragraph Spacing *2, 4, 5*
Password Protection *126, 127*
Password Security *126, 128, 150*
Picture *15, 23, 34, 38, 39, 40, 41, 42, 43, 44, 45, 50, 72, 150, 153*
PowerPoint Presentation from a Word Document *18, 148*

Q

Quick Access Toolbar *90, 91, 102, 103, 125*
Quick Part *64, 65*
Quick Style *18, 19, 20, 21*

R

Recolor *42, 43*
Regroup *48*
Reject Changes *137*
Replace *108, 109, 110, 111, 114*
Replace Text as You Type *114*
Resize *40*
Reviewing Pane *133*
Rotate *40, 41*
Ruler *8*

S

Section Break *68, 69, 73*
Send Backward *47*
Send to Back *46, 47*
Shading *13, 14, 15, 16, 53, 54, 56, 58, 59, 60, 61, 150*
Shadow *44, 45, 53*
Signature *172*
Slides from Outline *149*
Sources *92, 94, 96*
Spacing *2, 3, 4*
Spellcheck *116, 118, 120*
Split Cells *58*
Status Bar *90, 102, 103*

Index **177**

Style   *18, 19, 20, 21, 22, 23, 28, 29, 39, 41, 44, 51, 52, 82, 85, 117, 118, 148, 149, 160, 167*

T

Table   *50, 51 54, 55, 56, 57, 58, 59, 60, 61, 62, 111, 113, 151, 169*
Table Borders   *56, 59, 61*
Table of Authorities   *98, 100, 101*
Table of Contents   *50, 64, 78, 82, 83, 84, 85*
Table of Figures   *50, 51*
Table Properties   *55, 56*
Tab Stops   *6, 8*
Template   *21, 52, 55, 63, 64, 100, 104, 105, 106, 107, 123, 129, 162*
Text Alignment   *6, 8*
Text Box   *37, 47, 48, 52, 53, 64*
Text Wrapping   *39, 41, 46, 47*
Theme   *26, 27, 28, 30, 31, 91*
Track Changes   *134, 135, 137, 168, 170*
Transparent Color   *43*
Typeface   *165*

U

Ungroup   *46, 48*

V

View Side by Side   *138*

W

Watermark   *32, 33, 34, 35, 46*
Widows   *4, 5*
Widows and Orphans   *4*
WordArt   *36, 37*
Word Count   *175*
Word Options   *90, 102, 112, 114, 116, 118, 119, 120, 125, 151, 158, 159, 161*
Wrapping   *39, 41, 46, 47*